SURVIVING
in a
MATERIAL
WORLD

SURVIVING

in a

MATERIAL WORLD

The Lived Experience
of People in Poverty

RONALD PAUL HILL

University of Notre Dame Press
Notre Dame, Indiana

Manufactured in the United States of America

The author gratefully acknowledges permission to reprint material from the following sources:
Chapter 2: "What It's Like," written by Erik Schrody, published by T-Boy Music LLC/Irish
　　Intellect Music. Copyright © 2000.
Chapter 3: "Alone" from *Oh Pray My Wings Are Going to Fit Me Well* by Maya Angelou,
　　copyright © 1975 by Maya Angelou. Used by permission of Random House, Inc.
Chapter 4: "Little Boy" by Debra Lynn Stephens, published by permission of Debra Lynn
　　Stephens.
Chapter 5: "Dear Mama" from Tupak.
Chapter 6: Lines from "In the Good Old Days (When Times Were Bad)" by Dolly Parton,
　　reprinted by permission of Dolly Parton.
Chapter 8: "Dow Jones" by Vimal by permission of Vimal K. Jairath.

Library of Congress Cataloging-in-Publication Data
Hill, Ronald Paul.
　Surviving in a material world : the lived experience of people in
poverty / Ronald Paul Hill.
　　　p.　cm.
　Includes bibliographical references and index.
　　ISBN 0-268-04101-6 (alk. paper) —ISBN 0-268-04102-4 (pbk. : alk. paper)
　　　1. Poor—United States.　2. Poverty—United States.　3. Low-income
consumers—United States.　4. Poor—Australia.　5. Australian Aborigines—
Economic conditions.　I. Title.
HV91 .H53　2001
305.5'69'0973—dc21

　　　　　　　　　　　　　　　　　　　　　　　　　2001001937

∞ *This book is printed on acid-free paper.*

TO DEBRA LYNN

*So many talents
and so willing to share!*

Contents

ONE

Introduction to the World of Poverty

Living in a Material World

A wide variety of social scientists has investigated the topic of consumption over several generations. From the sociology of consuming to psychological perspectives of consumer decision making, these disciplines have developed a rich body of literature that helps business organizations, nonprofits, government agencies, and consumer advocates understand the rationale behind *why people buy*. One effect of this burgeoning literature was the founding of the Association for Consumer Research twenty-five years ago, an eclectic group of scholars from economics, psychology, sociology, anthropology, consumer sciences, and marketing. This group established the prestigious *Journal of Consumer Research* as an outlet for top-quality work in this interdisciplinary area, and it has remained at the forefront of thinking about consumer behavior since its inception.

Through the years, topics of inquiry have included processing of information contained in commercial promotions, decision making in the face of a number of distinct alternatives/choices, use of goods and services once they are acquired, and dispossession of what remains after a product's useful life has been exhausted. The underlying theme of most of this research is that there is *too much*. There is *too much* information to process efficiently and effectively, *too many* choices to evaluate, select from among, and use,

1

and *too much* waste when we have finished consuming. Thus, the material lives that are chronicled within this research stream are of the fortunate ones within our global community whose relative affluence places them in the enviable position of meeting most of their needs and desires on a regular basis.

While this perspective may be appropriate for the majority of citizens in the United States, it fails to characterize a significant minority, here as well as abroad. Approximately 12 percent of the population in this country lives in poverty, totaling about 32 million Americans. The poverty rate for children alone is even worse, with nearly one in five young people living in homes without adequate income or access to affordable rents, nutritious foods, and proper health care. Globally, the statistics are numbing: about one-third of the developing world, or 1.3 billion human beings, survive on less than the equivalent of one dollar a day. Many of these people are illiterate, lack safe drinking water, go to sleep hungry each night, and are unable to receive any health services.

The material lives of such individuals are markedly different from those of the affluent population characterized in the consumer-behavior literature. Instead of abundance and *too much*, their existence is defined by restriction and *too little*. For example, the poor face significant income barriers and logistical problems that severely limit their ability to acquire a wide range of needed and desired goods and services. The consequences of these restrictions typically are negative and may include separation and alienation from the primary consumer culture, feelings of loss of control over the consumption aspects of their lives, and poor mental and physical health. Nonetheless, the impoverished cope with these circumstances through a variety of emotional and behavioral strategies. From the perspective of a typical middle-class consumer these strategies may not make sense, but within the context of a restricted consumer existence, their use becomes easier to understand.

Over the course of the last decade, I have dedicated much of my research effort to answering the following question: How do various subpopulations among the poor survive in our material world? I began this scholarly voyage of discovery by examining how the homeless who live outside the social welfare system acquire and consume basic commodities. From there I moved to an investigation of homeless women and their children who are dependent upon shelters for their lodging, food, and clothing. My next subject was poor children who are incarcerated for property crimes that they committed in order to feast at the material table presented to them by the media. Portrayals of welfare mothers during the most recent round of welfare reform provided my next research direction, and I examined the extent to which the stereotypes advanced by both ends of the political spectrum represent the lived experience of such women and their children. Investigating the material existence of the rural poor was a natural subsequent step, and the focus of this study was on the provision of health care. The final context involved global poverty among indigenous people whose culture was disrupted and where material lives were shattered by European invaders.

Six Poverty Subpopulations

These six groups are the focus of this book. Each of the next six chapters is organized similarly. The chapter opens with a brief description of my scholarly research conducted with a particular subpopulation in order to give the reader grounding in empirical findings. The text then moves to a short story that employs internal dialogue and thick contextual description to provide a vivid portrait of the lived experience of a member of this group. The chapter closes with suggested readings that illuminate important aspects of the material lives of this subpopulation.

Chapter 2 chronicles the trials and tribulations of Jack, a man who recently became homeless. He spends his first night homeless in a municipal shelter but finds the experience threatening and demoralizing. He moves outside, living under a bridge on a landing until arsonists destroy his possessions, and then into a homeless community that resembles the shantytowns of the Great Depression. His final residence is an abandoned building that he shares discreetly with two other homeless men. Over time his vision of what constitutes a "home" evolves as he scales down his material goods to basic necessities. He does not thrive from the perspective of the dominant material culture, but he remains independent.

Chapter 3 describes the experience of homelessness of Zoë and her family. After a difficult childhood, Zoë becomes pregnant for a second time and moves in with the father of her younger child. Unfortunately, his employer reduces his work status to part-time, and they must leave their modest home. After a series of stays with relatives, Zoë and her children are forced to live in a variety of shelters, where many of their original possessions are lost and new ones are obtained. By the end of the story their circumstances have not improved, and they have run out of viable housing options. Zoë's emotional coping strategies are pushed to the breaking point.

Chapter 4 profiles the life of Fast Eddie, an older teen who lives in a poor community. Eddie grows up in an unstable environment where he is forced to move from one residence to another during his early childhood. His father is a distant and violent man who comes in and out of his life. His mother is warm and caring but submissive, and Eddie takes advantage of her nature as he matures into a teenager. Over time his relationship to material possessions goes from joyful anticipation to apathy to anger at his relative poverty. Eddie falls in with a fast crowd, and they eventually commit property crimes in order to gain access to the material world. He eventually is caught, punished, and returned to society. However, a lack of opportunity causes him to drift back slowly toward a life of crime.

Chapter 5 is about Anita and her children and their existence on welfare. Anita struggles as a child of a welfare mother and vows not to live that life. However, her existence takes a radical turn when she becomes pregnant as a teenager, quits school, and marries. The first few years of this union go smoothly, and her family grows to five people. Unfortunately, though, her husband's employer lays him off, and the only viable option for a new job is out of town. The husband takes the position and works diligently but is fired after a physical confrontation with his boss, leaving Anita without much income. She eventually joins the welfare rolls, only to find that the level of support is too low for her family to survive. Nonetheless, she copes by learning how to navigate the welfare system and even gets her high school diploma and some clerical training along the way. In the end she wonders whether she and her family can make it on their own without any external support.

Chapter 6 centers on Tammy and her mother and their lives in a former coal-mining town near the Appalachian Mountains. When Tammy was a youngster, her family had most of what they needed to get by. However, by the time Tammy's own children were young adults, the mines had closed permanently and the financial basis of the town had collapsed. Jobs became scarce, and supporting services in the town dried up. Tammy's mother eventually became ill, and they were unable to get adequate medical attention within a reasonable distance from their home. Alternative care from medical professionals who operated a mobile health unit eventually provided aid that was grounded in the community spirit of these rural people.

Chapter 7 examines the world of Mary and her maternal ancestors, Aboriginal people who lived most of their lives in a remote region of the Australian Outback. Mary rebels against her cultural heritage and marries a white man in order to partake in the material world that exists outside of her homeland. However, over time Mary realizes the importance of her identity as an Aborigine, and she returns home to live among her people following the death of her mother. She works tirelessly to bring cultural renewal to them and to seek Aboriginal ways of living in a white society. The community experiences many successes, but the long-term survival of their ancient way of life remains in doubt.

Some Relevant Questions

The choice of these six different poverty subpopulations and the development of chapters based on them lead to a number of interesting questions. For instance, are most or all important subpopulations covered in this volume? The answer is a qualified "maybe." From a domestic perspective, the six groups provide an adequate range of the differentiated impoverished subpopulations within the United States. However, rural poverty is more varied than presented here, and coverage could be expanded to include a number of other geographical locations such as the Mississippi Delta, Missouri Ozarks, the Timber Region of the Pacific Northwest, and rural California. For the individual interested in exploring these regions, the suggested readings are an excellent start. Additionally, global poverty is more differentiated than any short story involving a single country could detail, especially when one considers how poverty is manifested in areas of the world like sub-Saharan Africa, Eastern Europe, and South Asia. Once again, the suggested readings provide a solid introduction.

A second relevant question asks, Are these portraits research-driven or are they fictional accounts? The answer is "both." I have taken great pains to ensure that every aspect of these people's material lives is drawn directly from research published in peer-reviewed journals. The most important parts of my research stream which inform each chapter are summarized for the reader's review prior to the short story, and I urge interested parties to examine these works more carefully. However, many of the nonmaterial aspects of these lives are imaginatively recreated to give a more complete picture of their existence. Nonetheless, I believe that such people exist within the contexts described and that an accurate depiction of their lives is presented.

A third question concerns the vulnerability of the people portrayed in this volume: In what ways have the identity and integrity of the poor been protected? One answer involves a careful look at the short stories themselves. In every story, the totality of incidents discussed, the emotions expressed, and the behaviors manifested is a composite of the experiences of many different people rather than a description of the life of a single identifiable individual. Further, I have done my best in these portraits to avoid creating new stereotypes by presenting a wide variety of circumstances and subsequent reactions that defy easy categorization of the focal character or his or her significant others. To these same ends, no dialogue is provided to avoid turns of phrase that might be associated with a particular race or region or would allow a particular person to be recognized.

A final question results from the gendered and Catholic natures of these stories. For example, in four of the six composites the focal character is female. On the surface, this may look like some form of gender bias, but in truth poverty throughout the world has disproportionately affected women, especially within the contexts selected for this book. Additionally, four of the six chapters mention the Catholic Church in some capacity. Given the Church's commitment to social justice and its support of vulnerable populations such as the impoverished, no one should be surprised that its institutions play a visible role in these environments. Further, my affiliation with Catholic universities over the last decade has allowed me access to such institutions and those they serve, significantly influencing the direction of my research.

Closing Remarks

My primary goal in writing this book has been to make the material lives of the poor accessible to a wide audience of students, researchers, professionals, and other interested parties, regardless of educational field or background. To accomplish this objective, I needed to find a format that would allow me to communicate this information without using technical language or discipline-specific jargon. After extensive work in this area and years of reflection, I decided that the short story seemed like a logical best choice. During the pursuit of my research, I developed these composites informally for other purposes as I struggled to understand the world of people in poverty. This vehicle seems like a natural extension of my understanding of the poor, and I can almost see the faces of the main characters as I read these stories a final time.

A secondary purpose of this book is to help rid society of the common stereotypes that exist about nearly all of the subpopulations covered in this volume. From the homeless man who begs by the subway station to the welfare mother in the urban ghetto, our society has responded to the visible aspects of their lives with harsh criticism. We make these evaluations based on what little we know about them from our own viewpoint, rather than seeing a complete picture of their lives from their own perspectives. We assume that they have parents, teachers, and civic and community organizations and resources that mirror our own. Our solutions to their dilemmas often are equally naive: *Why don't they just get a job?* I hope this book makes clear that such approaches fail to reflect the lived world of such people and the restrictions they endure in the face of the American consumption dream.

After the composites are presented, chapter 8 examines the similarities across all impoverished subpopulations and provides a gestalt of the poor in their totality. With these characteristics in mind, I present solutions that attack the roots of poverty through an understanding of the strengths and weaknesses of these six subpopulations. I attempt to move the discussion beyond the views of the poor as either helpless victims of a cruel world or as corrupt people responsible for their own fate. The book closes with a bibliography of valuable readings that guided my work over the years.

TWO

Hidden Homeless
The Trials
and Tribulations of Jack

We've all seen the man at the liquor store beggin' for your change.
The hair on his face is dirty, dreadlocked and full of mange.
He ask the man for what he could spare with shame in his eyes.
Get a job you f——in' slob's all he replied.

God forbid you ever had to walk a mile in his shoes
'Cause then you really might know what it's like to sing the blues...
—Everlast, "What It's Like"

As a result of persistent unemployment among the poor, deinstitutionalization of the mentally ill, substance abuse and addiction, and scarcity of low-cost housing, homelessness in the United States increased throughout the 1980s and into the 1990s. The homeless often were defined by their lack of shelter that meets minimal health and safety standards. However, more recent work suggests that this view is too narrow since it fails to consider a host of other unmet needs with regard to goods and services such as food, clothing, and medical care.

The focus of this chapter is on the "hidden homeless," a poverty subgroup that lives outside the social welfare system. These people consistently disparage the services available to the homeless and claim that reliance on the organizations that provide them, especially public shelters, reduces self-esteem. Thus, they attempt to live by their own resources and through use of their own abilities rather than submit to institutional control.

For the hidden homeless, acquiring possessions involves activities that are markedly different from those of the typical consumer in our society. First, access to traditional outlets for products, such as supermarkets or restaurants, often is restricted for the homeless because of financial or hygiene factors, dress requirements, and interpersonal problems. Second, many of the necessities of life—food, clothing, and materials for shelter—are scavenged from the refuse of others rather than purchased. Third, the homeless engage in nontraditional employment or income-producing strategies that require unconventional methods for the acquisition of marketable items.

Portions of the chapter concentrate on scavenging activities that take up many of the waking hours of the hidden homeless. Such activities involve the search for partially consumed products, with homeless persons as secondary consumers. Much scavenging takes place in public garbage cans or Dumpsters, which hold up to twenty cubic yards of material. Uninformed observers may think that homeless persons aimlessly search such receptacles, but research reveals that those who scavenge often are adept at acquiring useful items and employ developed methods of selection and search to improve the probability of finding goods like edible food and clothing. Additionally, scavenging is used to make money through recycling of cans and bottles, scrap metal, car parts, and building materials.

Scavenging also plays a role in the establishment of alternative living arrangements. Shelters are created out of abandoned automobiles, bridge abutments, condemned housing, and construction materials. These "homes" may be nontraditional, but they often involve some form of community with others, from loosely aligned individuals who are aware of each other's presence but interact infrequently, to thriving cooperatives with daily communication. The former are referred to as "shadow communities" because of the limited mode of relationship, while the latter are reminiscent of the shantytowns that sprang up during the Great Depression.

THE TRIALS AND TRIBULATIONS
OF JACK

The Road to Homelessness

Jack woke up in the back seat of his 1981 Ford Mustang, which was parked at the end of a street next to a neighborhood park. His memory of the events of the previous evening was kind of fuzzy. He had been living, temporarily, with a friend he had known since high school. He lost his apartment last year, and his parents tired of his "behavior problems" after about ten months and kicked him out. His friend Tim was his last hope.

Jack remembered seeing Tim's wife come out of the bathroom after her shower yesterday afternoon. He was lying on their couch, finishing the last few bottles of a twelve-pack of beer he had purchased earlier that day. Jack said something to her that he thought was somewhat clever, but she reacted by turning around and locking herself in the bathroom. When Tim came home a few minutes later, he told Jack it was time for him to leave.

The scene that followed was typical of Jack's three-week stay with his old friend. They screamed and yelled at each other for about thirty minutes, and Jack said some things about Tim's wife that he later regretted. However, unlike previous fights in which they made up in the end and decided to give living together one more try, Tim insisted that Jack go immediately.

Jack decided to leave his car parked where it was for the time being. He was low on gas and down to his last few dollars. Hunger was beginning to set in as his mind began to clear, and he started out on foot toward a neighborhood convenience store three blocks away. Before departing, he made sure the trunk, which housed his remaining possessions, was locked securely. He also locked the doors to the car after neatly folding the blankets he used the previous night to keep himself warm.

The weather was surprisingly crisp and cool for a late September morning, and Jack pondered getting his one remaining jacket from the car. In the end he decided against it, hoping the air might clear the alcoholic fog from his head. As he walked along his thoughts turned to the future—where he would live, how he would eat, and what he would do to make money over time. After a few moments he drove such thoughts from his head and focused on the here-and-now.

As he entered the store, the cashier looked up immediately and gave him an unfriendly stare. Jack had been here several times in the last few months and was unfazed by such treatment. As he passed a number of other patrons on his way to the coffee and day-old doughnuts, they seemed to back away from him and turn the other direction. Nonetheless, Jack was undeterred in his morning quest for a pick-me-up, and he answered their avoidance with a cocky strut.

As he approached the front of the store to get some cigarettes and pay his bill, a man Jack recognized as the owner came toward him from a small office next to the cash register. He introduced himself as Bill and politely asked if he could speak with Jack privately outside. Jack was confused by his request but agreed, taking his coffee and doughnuts with him.

Once outdoors, Bill proceeded to ask Jack to refrain from entering his store again. He noted that the other customers had complained about Jack's appearance and mannerisms, and Bill explained that he was afraid some of them might not return. He told Jack to keep the coffee and doughnuts, as well as a carton of Camels he had in his hands, as a parting goodwill gesture. Jack was confused and angered by this discussion, and he responded with a menacing growl as he grabbed the carton of cigarettes and quickly walked away.

Without anywhere in particular to go, he headed for the park so that he could walk off his emotions and decide what to do next. After about an hour of walking and swearing, Jack sat down on a bench to digest his food and have a smoke. As he lit the first Camel of the day, he took some pride in getting the carton for free. If he was careful and smoked them down to the filter, they would last a long while.

Now what? His parents were out. His older brother had made sure of that by having them get a restraining order that barred him from calling and asking for money. His only other sibling, a sister, had moved to another state two years ago, and he hadn't spoken with her since her departure. Tim and the rest of his childhood friends were useless. Even the church he had attended since birth had turned against him.

His thoughts changed to daydreams of better times. He drifted back to his school years over a decade ago, and the good times with his old buddies. Unlike today, with their concentration on jobs and families, his time with them in those days was spent looking for the next party.

Jack was interrupted sometime later when a group of joggers ran past. He noticed that the day was slipping away and that he was no closer to a solution to his problems. Maybe he should go back to his car and take a drive, but where would he go? He needed food, money, and a place to stay, and he had run out of options for all three.

He remembered a conversation he had had with his parents when they threw him out. His mother, in tears at the time, had handed him a piece of paper with the name and address of a public shelter in town for homeless men. Jack was insulted by the gesture but stuffed the note in his pocket anyway. It was now in the glove compartment of his car, and he thought he might take a quick look at it.

Jack got up and began the short walk to where his car was located. As he approached, he noticed that someone in the house next to where he was parked was looking out the window at him—so much for his right to privacy. Somebody was bound to call the police if he stayed another night, so he started the car and moved up the street.

Almost as a reflex, he reached for the glove box in search of the shelter's address. Jack noticed that he had less than a quarter tank of gas but, after determining the location, surmised that he could easily reach his destination. He was nervous about what he might find there, but he knew the shelter was just a short-term fix until he could sort things out.

From Shelter Living to Living Outside

After driving for twenty-five minutes, Jack located the shelter on the corner of a busy intersection in a run-down neighborhood. He looked for a place to park on the street or in an empty lot, but nothing was to be found. Jack began circling the blocks in the vicinity until he discovered a spot. It was about a quarter mile away on a side street that did not get much daytime traffic, so he was unlikely to get a ticket or be towed for parking illegally. He could see three other cars nearby that were up on cinder blocks with their tires and engines removed, but he paid them little attention. Jack had nothing of real value to anyone but himself in the car, and the automobile itself was nearly twenty years old.

After parking as close to the curb as possible, he got out and locked the doors. Jack proceeded to open the trunk and look at his meager belongings to decide what to bring with him. Everything he owned was stuffed into two large plastic trash bags. Most of their contents were clothing of one kind or another, with a few pictures, books, and important papers rounding out his load. The only thing he decided to remove was his birth certificate. If someone at the shelter asked for identification, that was all he had since he had lost his driver's license and Social Security card a few months back.

As he approached the shelter, Jack noticed several men milling around in front as if they were waiting for the doors to open. He went up to ring the bell or knock but was abruptly told by one of the men that no one would answer until 6:00 P.M. Another man pointed to the back of a loosely formed line and said Jack should wait his turn.

About ninety minutes after he arrived, the doors opened and the men hurriedly entered the shelter. Jack observed what the men in front of him were doing—signing in next to an assigned bunk number and taking a card from a clerk with an uninterested look on his face. When it was his turn, Jack followed their lead and then headed into the adjoining room.

This room was the dining area, and it contained a distinct smell of body odor mixed with sour milk. Jack waited in line to be served, and, when his turn came, he was handed a tray containing a boiled hot dog on a bun, some macaroni salad, a dinner roll, and a gelatin cup with fruit. As he continued in the procession, he was given a Styrofoam cup of coffee and a piece of sponge cake for dessert.

Jack walked over to a table where seven men sat quietly and placed his tray in front of the last seat on the bench. The man next to him looked over but said nothing. Across the table, another man was making the sign of the cross each time he placed food in his mouth. Jack made a mental note to avoid him in the future.

As unappetizing as the meal looked, Jack was hungry and willing to give it a try. The hot dog had an oily taste as if it had been cooked too long with others of its kind. The macaroni salad had a tangy flavor, and he pushed it away out of fear that it might be spoiled. The roll was hard but edible, and the gelatin was taste-less. By the time Jack got around to it, the coffee was lukewarm. The sponge cake was growing mold on one side.

Once he finished eating what he could, Jack leaned back and placed a Camel in his mouth. As he struck a match to light up, one of the kitchen crew came running over to tell him not to smoke in the dining room. Such activity was allowed only in the game room between 7:00 P.M. and 9:00 P.M. If he had to smoke now, Jack would have to leave the shelter but he would not be able to return until tomorrow.

Jack sullenly looked down at his tray, angered by such disre-spect. Why were they treating him like a child? Even his parents let him come and go as he pleased once he was in high school. As his thoughts shifted to dinners at home and higher-quality meals, someone announced it was time for the men to bus their own trays and move into the common areas. The men stood almost in unison, placed their half-eaten meals on nearby carts, and moved into the hallway.

Jack had his choice of three different rooms, and he selected the one with a sign hanging over the doorway that read SMOKING ALLOWED. He immediately lit up as he entered the room, and the space was quickly filled to capacity. After a few minutes, the air was so thick with smoke it was hard to see the exit. There were few conversations among the men, and Jack contented himself with staring straight ahead and allowing his eyes to focus on nothing at all.

Three cigarettes later and with his nicotine "fix" complete, Jack decided to explore the other rooms. The dominant feature of one was an old black-and-white TV with a coat hanger for an antenna. People seemed to be staring at it without noticing what was on, which was a rerun of the old *Happy Days* sitcom. No one seemed to be laughing or enjoying it, but the sign above the television announced that changing the channel was forbidden.

The third room contained a rack of ancient magazines with torn covers and several pages removed. There was also a table with a Bible in the center. This room was the only one with couches and chairs, so Jack plopped down in the remaining empty seat. He picked up a magazine to browse, but lost interest when he saw that the lead article was about vacation destinations. He then closed his eyes and let his mind drift.

After some time had passed, Jack heard an announcement in the hall that the "guests" had fifteen minutes before bedtime. He wasn't sure what that meant, but he felt certain it would be his last chance that evening to have a cigarette. Jack hurried into the game room and lit up quickly, deeply inhaling each drag for maximum effect.

At exactly 9:00 P.M. by the large clock on the wall, the men began a slow march down a different hallway toward a large cavernous room containing a sea of beds stacked three high. Their movements reminded Jack of movies he had seen during his youth where cowboys herded cattle into pens. As the men entered, they moved in different directions in search of their beds. He had number 162, a bottom bunk near the middle of the room.

He climbed in immediately and quickly surmised that the flat pillow and thin blanket were adequate but far from ideal. As his thoughts moved from his current surroundings to why he had come here in the first place, an unsteady man, who was drunk, stoned, or both, interrupted his reverie by stepping on his arm on the way to the middle bunk. Jack hoped he would quickly fall asleep and that the man above him would settle down in a drug-induced stupor.

An hour later the lights were turned off without warning, and the room was plunged into darkness. After a few moments, Jack's eyes adjusted, and he noticed that a tiny bit of light seeped in through the six barred windows near the ceiling. He tried to concentrate on someplace else, and he pondered the relative security of his old room in his parents' home.

Jack was awakened sometime later by a shrill scream coming from his left. Other men nearby started yelling at the screamer to shut up but to no avail. After about fifteen minutes of incessant high-pitched noise, two men entered the room, grabbed the screamer by his arms, and dragged him out of his bed and into the hallway.

Jack's bunkmate began to stir as a result of this commotion, and then leaned over the side of his bed and vomited. Some of the vomit splattered up on Jack and his bedding as it hit the floor and rebounded. Jack began to feel queasy himself, and he turned to the other side of the bed, closed his eyes tightly, and vowed to get out of this place as soon as he could.

A loud bell sounded; Jack looked at the clock and saw it was 6:00 A.M. He got up out of his bed and stretched in an attempt to wake himself. He glanced up at his bunkmate, who was snoring loudly, oblivious to the movement around him. Jack shook his head in disgust and followed the line of men out the door toward the dining area.

Breakfast was similar in quality to dinner—runny scrambled eggs, the same kind of roll as at the last meal, and coffee. Jack picked at the eggs, downed the roll followed by his coffee, and headed for the door. As he was leaving, one of the kitchen crew shouted that he could not return until 6:00 P.M. Jack turned, defiantly placed a Camel in his mouth, and told the worker in no uncertain terms that he would rather die on the streets than come back.

Upon leaving, he turned left in search of his car. As he rounded the corner of the block on which he believed it was parked, Jack stopped and stared in amazement. His auto was where he had left it, but the windows on the passenger side were smashed and someone had written a graffiti tag on the hood. He approached the car tentatively and looked inside. Glass was everywhere. His blankets were gone, and the radio had been ripped out of the dashboard.

He opened the driver's side door and began brushing the glass onto the street with his bare hands. Jack cut himself twice and started cursing loudly. Two teenagers walking by snickered at his troubles, and they began mimicking his diatribe under their breath.

He started the car, pulled away from the curb, and shouted obscenities as loudly as he could into the air. He was headed nowhere in particular, but he knew he wanted to get away from this place. As Jack drove along, rage filled his entire body. He had been treated like a child, fed like a dog, herded like a cow, and vomited on by a drug addict. His car had been vandalized, and his net worth had shrunk proportionately. He could think of nothing good about this experience.

Jack realized that shelters were not for him. The people who inhabited shelters were the truly desperate—unable to fend for themselves and without hope. He was *not* like them. He would find a way to survive by his own wits and abilities, and he would live life according to his own rules.

He looked down at the gas gauge and realized he had less than one-eighth of a tank left. Jack opened his wallet and saw that he had only $4.78 in cash, barely enough to cover a decent lunch. Just then, he caught sight of a CARS FOR CASH sign, and he made an abrupt turn into the adjoining parking lot.

After about ten minutes of stilted discussion, a man wearing a cheap polyester suit offered Jack fifty dollars for his car. Jack felt the bid was ridiculously low for his most valuable asset, but the man insisted he would pay no more. Jack signaled his disdain with a loud huffing sound as he signed the appropriate papers. He gave the car one final glance, removed the two bags of his belongings from the trunk, and walked away. At least he would eat what he wanted for a few days.

After some reflection, Jack decided to head back to the park in his old neighborhood. He could hide out under the bridge that spanned the river, bisecting a large wooded area. If his memory from childhood was correct, there was a ladder next to where the bank dropped off that led to a landing. He could use some of his remaining clothes for bedding, and he would have a good hiding place for the rest of his possessions when he had to go in search of food.

His new home was about five miles away. He stopped and lit another Camel, and he hoisted the bags over his shoulders. They weren't particularly heavy, but he knew they would seem weighty after a while. Unfortunately, he had no other way to transport them, so he decided to move slowly to conserve his energy.

After walking three miles, he came upon a large supermarket. Jack thought he might go in and get a few things to eat and drink for the next several days, but he was confused about what to do with his bags. If he left them outside, they might be stolen or accidentally thrown out by a store employee. However, if he carried them inside, someone might get suspicious that he was stealing.

In the end, he carried them inside and tucked them carefully behind a row of shopping carts. He figured they would go unnoticed only for a few minutes, so he planned to move quickly through the store. Jack concentrated his attention on food and drink that came in plastic wrapping or containers and would not spoil. Such goods were lighter, more convenient, and easily stored. If he was right, he had only a few cubic feet for storage once his bedding was laid.

His bill came to $26.45, almost half his cash. However, Jack estimated that he could live on these groceries for five days, if necessary. He left the store and found his two bundles undisturbed. He divided his food and drink evenly between the two bags, lit another Camel, and continued on his journey.

From Living Outside to Communal Living

When Jack finally arrived at his destination, it was as he remembered it. Tall trees ran down to the bank of the river and surrounded the bridge. No one lived in the area since it was public property, and access on foot was difficult. There was a metal ladder attached to the bridge which protruded from the side, extending from highway level to the landing that would be his home.

Jack was concerned about how best to approach the landing with his two bags. He decided to take them down one at a time, and he waited behind a tall tree until the road was empty to avoid detection. After about five minutes the highway cleared, and he made a mad dash for the ladder. With his pack slung over his back like Santa Claus, he hoisted himself over the top rung and quickly descended the ten steps to the landing. He came back up for the second bag a few minutes later, using similar speed and stealth.

Once he had everything he owned with him, Jack began the process of creating a livable environment. The landing itself was about twenty feet long, with a retaining wall covering the last eight. He decided to place everything he owned within the covered area in case someone else ventured down the steps.

Jack positioned eight pieces of clothing along a six-foot stretch of the interior for bedding. He hoped it would be sufficient insulation from the cold concrete. On top he laid the only blanket he had left, along with the two small pillows that were all that remained of his apartment's living room. The rest of his things he placed in one bag, and he stored the food by itself in the other. Both were situated at the end of his bed as a buffer against the outside world.

Satisfied with his work, Jack sat on the landing next to his new home and lit a Camel. He contemplated the plunging temperatures and what they suggested about the coming winter. Jack thought he had enough clothing and bedding to survive the fall, but the really cold months—December, January, and February—would be a different story. Since there was nothing he could do about it now, Jack refocused his attention on his evening meal.

Dinner was made up of two peanut butter and jelly sandwiches, accompanied by a pack of Twinkies for dessert. He washed the whole meal down with a twenty-ounce bottle of cola and was thankful for the caffeine it contained. It wasn't a meal at a four-star restaurant, but Jack consoled himself with the belief that it was better than shelter food and he could eat it whenever he wanted.

The next several days were uneventful but for the early frost. Jack wrapped himself in every bit of clothing he owned that cold evening, but he still shivered all night. Also, he was now out of food and hesitant about his next move. A trip to the store would surely drain his cash reserves, and he would be forced to leave all of his things behind. After the incident with the car, he was worried that his meager possessions might be ransacked.

In the end, he decided he had no other option but to leave temporarily in search of food. He calmed himself by noting that no one had bothered him so far. Jack checked his wallet and found he had exactly $28.33. He put the money back in his wallet and placed it securely in his front pocket. Then he climbed up the ladder, waited for traffic to clear, and jumped up onto the highway.

He decided to go back to the supermarket he had patronized during his last shopping trip. Jack made a mental note of what he needed this time. He still had enough toilet paper and toothpaste for the only hygiene activities available to him now. The peanut butter and jelly had worked out okay, but the bread had gotten a bit hard over time. Drinks were cold enough—maybe too cold. A hot cup of coffee or soup would be nice but was impossible.

Jack entered the market at a brisk pace and grabbed a hand-held basket rather than a shopping cart. If he couldn't carry his items in the store, there was no way he would be able to transport them home. He concentrated on foods that were wrapped in single-serving portions. While they were probably more expensive, such foodstuffs were less likely to go stale over time. The cashier charged him $23.50 for the load, and Jack made a mental note that he had $4.83 left, about the same amount he had started with before selling his car.

On his way back home, he lit a Camel and strolled at a leisurely pace. Things weren't so bad. Despite the cold he was glad for the time alone and the ability to live life according to *his* desires. His parents had been demanding, and the shelter was worse. For the first time in a long time, Jack was truly on his own.

When he gained sight of the bridge, he noticed that a car was parked about fifty feet from the ladder. He approached it carefully and looked inside. It was neither a police nor a highway commission vehicle, and that realization caused Jack to breathe a sigh of relief. However, as he advanced toward the ladder, he heard sounds of conversation and laughter coming from below.

He called down from the highway to the people who now occupied his home. They quieted immediately, and Jack could smell the faint odor of marijuana rising from below. This invasion and the possible loss of his possessions frightened him, and he cursed himself for leaving them behind. After a few moments his fear turned to anger, and he got up the courage to investigate the situation. He placed his food behind a large tree about ten feet into the woods, and he ran down the steps to the landing.

The intruders were three male teens dressed in the latest hip-hop fashions. They stared at Jack in disbelief as if they were looking at a circus freak. Jack decided he should move quickly while he had them off-guard, and he told them in no uncertain terms that this was *his* home and they must leave now. One grinned slyly at Jack after these remarks, while the other two looked menacingly at him.

They exchanged harsh words for a few minutes, neither side wanting to back down. Jack started growling like a wild animal protecting its young, and he clenched his fists, ready to pounce. The three intruders glanced at each other uncertainly, and then one of them jumped to the ladder and ran up the stairs. The other two panicked when their leader abandoned them, and they quickly followed suit.

Jack examined his bedding and saw that it was disheveled but intact. The two bags were untouched, and he quickly surmised that the overall damage to his home was minimal. Nonetheless, Jack felt violated and vulnerable. If these kids could find his hiding place, how long would it take for others to follow?

He lit a Camel and took a deep drag, hoping to calm his nerves. He wished he had something to drink containing alcohol, but he realized he couldn't afford it. After several hours of smok-

ing and obsessing about how to protect himself and his possessions, Jack crawled into bed for a fitful night's sleep.

He dreamed that the three boys had been assigned the role of
his torturers by the devil. He had died and gone straight to hell
because of his evil deeds on earth, and he was tied down with
chains over hot coals. Each of the boys had a long whip, and they
took turns lashing him. As the whip cracked down on his body,
the torturer would announce in a righteous tone the name of
someone Jack had wronged during his lifetime. Jack looked across
his bloody body at the faces of his tormenters and discovered that
the boys had transformed into his father, brother, and sister.

He awoke several times that night in a cold sweat despite the
cool temperatures. Jack was uncertain about the meaning of the
dream, and he became increasingly troubled and agitated. When
dawn finally arrived, he was glad to be rid of this nightmare. He
forced himself to think of other things, lit a Camel, and prepared
breakfast.

Over the next several days Jack did very little, and he left
home only one time to retrieve his packages from the woods. By
the end of the week, his provisions were nearly exhausted and the
nighttime temperatures were almost unbearable. He began to despair and even contemplated suicide a few times. In the end, he
decided to buy a forty-ounce bottle of malt liquor with his remaining cash and try to forget his worries for at least one night.

As he walked toward the only liquor store within three miles,
Jack wondered what day it was. Without a regular routine to keep
him focused on time, the days seemed to run together in an endless chain. He thought it was probably Monday or Tuesday in
early October. He made a mental note to check the calendar in
the store.

Jack entered the establishment from the back door, moved to
the beer display on his left, and made a selection. There was a sale
on a particular brand, and he was able to purchase two bottles of
malt liquor with his remaining funds. He was pleased with his
luck until he realized that he now had exactly twenty-one cents to
his name.

He opened one bottle and drained it on his way home. Evening had turned to night, and the temperature began to plummet. Jack noticed that it didn't bother him as much as usual, and he gave thanks for the numbing influence of the liquor. His mood was beginning to brighten until he reached the bridge and saw a fire truck with the lights flashing next to the entrance to his home.

He ran at top speed and reached the bridge as the firefighters were finishing their work. They had received reports from several motorists of flames rising from under the bridge, but the blaze was nearly extinguished by the time they arrived. Two of them had climbed down the ladder and hosed down the area to make sure the fire was completely under control.

Jack said little in response to their words or actions, and they looked at him with a mixture of disgust and pity. He dropped down the ladder in a single leap only to find his clothes, bedding, and other possessions charred and soaked. As he picked through the remains on a salvage mission, he found several pieces of a broken bottle. Jack surmised that it had once contained gasoline or some other flammable liquid that must have started the fire in the first place. The most likely suspects for this act of arson were the teens he had run off a few days back.

All in all, he had two shirts, one pair of pants, a pillow, and some random socks that still could be used. They were completely soaked, so he spent the next few minutes wringing them out as best he could. He wrapped them into a bundle and laid them on the only dry spot on the landing. Jack then plopped down, opened the other bottle of liquor, and took a long swig.

Two hours later, with the bottle empty and exhaustion setting in, Jack rolled over and fell asleep. He didn't awaken until early the next morning, and he was glad to have slept through the night. As he reached for his last pack of Camels, he noticed that his hands were numb and shaking. He staggered to his feet and started running in place to get his blood pumping. Once the feeling returned to his extremities, he stopped moving and lit a cigarette.

What to do next? Clearly, he couldn't stay here. Even if the firefighters didn't inform the police of his presence, those kids could always return. Anyway, without his clothing and bedding, he would freeze to death in a few days. He had to leave, and now seemed like a good time. He stuffed the Camels in his pocket, picked up his bundle of clothes, and went up the ladder.

Jack decided to head back into the city. There was more going on in town and more opportunity to acquire the things he needed. After walking several miles, he came across a series of restaurants lined up like dominos along the street. They reminded him of how hungry he was, despite his situation. However, with only a few cents to his name, he was unlikely to be able to do much about it.

He walked around back behind the row of buildings, hoping to discover a doughnut or some other item that might have fallen from a delivery truck. Seeing none, he opened the lid of one of the Dumpsters in search of half-eaten or partially spoiled food that had at least some edible portions left. As he raised the metal top higher to get a better look inside, a voice came out of nowhere telling him he was wasting his time.

Jack looked quickly to his left and then to his right, and he discovered the source of the voice. About three bins down, he saw a small, disheveled man in a long coat wearing a stocking cap. He addressed Jack again, telling him that restaurants never discarded safe-to-eat foodstuffs in the morning. That only happened in the evenings. "Dumpster diving" was an art that Jack clearly was unaware of.

The man had just slept off a two-day drinking binge, and he was headed home. He lived in a makeshift town called Dicksonville, which was named for the mayor whose economic policies had led to the recent decline in housing for the poor. It was a community of people like Jack who banded together for support and protection. If Jack was quiet and listened carefully to the rules, he could come along for breakfast.

Communal Living and Scavenging for Possessions

As they walked along, his new companion told Jack about the people who lived in this homeless community. They were mostly single men, a few single women, and a couple of families. It was located on an abandoned exit ramp that was blocked on both ends by cement barriers. The police had come by a few times to check them out but left them alone since they found no evidence of illegal activity.

Some lived outside under the stars, but most had constructed their own homes out of materials scavenged from construction sites around the city. People respected each other's privacy, but they often shared food, drink, and extra clothing. While no formal authority existed to keep order, stealing, threatening behavior, or use of drugs resulted in swift expulsion by the group as a whole. Virtually everybody worked at some kind of job, from full-time employment to recycling of cans, bottles, and other salable items scavenged locally.

When they finally arrived at their destination, Jack was surprised at the sheer size of the community. It comprised fifteen separate dwellings, including lean-tos, tents, single-person abodes made of cardboard and plastic, and elaborate multiroom homes made of wood, brick, and Sheetrock. Music filled the air, and smoke rose from the tops of a few places indicating fires for heating or cooking.

Jack was introduced to some men standing around a kettle-drum preparing breakfast. Most nodded politely, and one even extended his hand to shake. Jack was a bit taken aback by this gesture of friendship, and he tried to remember the last time someone greeted him with respect. He slowly extended his hand and asked politely for some food. Jack was the first person served, and he sat down quietly at a picnic table next to the grill and began eating his meal with relish.

When he was done, he placed his paper plate in a large bin marked FOOD TRASH and his utensils in soapy water with other plastic forks, knives, and spoons. His new acquaintance then gave him a quick tour of the place, pointing out shared facilities where people went to relieve themselves or wash their clothing. Jack mentioned the wiring streaming down the side of the highway onto the ramp. His companion told him that an electrician had run the wire from the base of a lamppost to a community outlet so that they could use electrical appliances such as small refrigerators, hot plates, microwave ovens, televisions, and radios.

There was one place, in particular, that he wanted Jack to see. It was his home, which he shared with a woman he referred to as his "common-law bride." The exterior was made of stone and brick, held together with a substance that looked like clay. The structure contained three rooms with a small crawlspace between them. The roof was covered with black tar to protect the interior from rain or snow.

They entered through a door that was connected by hinges on one side and an interior clasp on the other. Jack's companion used a ten-penny nail to reach past the door and unhook the clasp, and the door popped open to allow them passage. Once inside, Jack was struck by how well lighted the interior was from the sun alone.

As they passed from room to room, Jack noticed that each chamber contained wall decorations, mementos, and religious art. This place had a homey feel that reminded Jack more of his family's residence than a makeshift shack. The largest of the three rooms housed a TV, a radio, a microwave oven, and their bed. The other two seemed like personalized spaces for each of them, with books, toiletries, sitting areas, and candles. In the center of the largest room was an old water heater with an opening on one side. His acquaintance explained that it was used to heat the house by burning things inside while allowing the smoke to escape through the top.

Over the next two months, Jack settled into the community, staking out some ground a few feet from his new friend. The interior skeleton of his home was composed of two-by-fours he picked up on the edge of town where some old rowhouses were being renovated. He felt badly about taking them, but he really had no choice if he was to survive the winter. The exterior was plywood covered with a clear plastic tarp. Jack insulated the whole structure with remnants he found behind a carpet store. He ran an electrical wire from the community extension to his home so that he could power a single light and a small space heater. Now, even when the temperature dropped below freezing, Jack remained comfortable.

His clothing, however, was a different story. Jack had lost most of his winter apparel in the fire, and he needed to replace it. To this end, he joined several members of the community on their weekly visits to a small, single-room house behind a private shelter where donated clothing was stored. Over time, Jack acquired two additional pairs of pants, three sweaters, a pair of work boots, two stocking caps, and an insulated jacket. They weren't the latest styles, but they would keep him warm.

Jack also mastered the art of scavenging for food and salable items. Along with others, he would rummage through the dumpsters of certain restaurants after closing time for leftovers. Jack learned to search for the heavier bags, since they were more likely to contain food. Items that were warm and untouched were valued the most. Jack was surprised to find that some of these establishments seemed to pack such foodstuffs purposefully in a single bag and place it carefully in the front of the bin. He quietly thanked them for their generosity. On occasion, when other sources were dry, someone would call a local takeout restaurant and place a large order. When no one came to retrieve it, the staffers often would throw the food out at closing time. Jack or someone else would then go and retrieve it.

Additionally, Jack learned to earn income for cigarettes and other necessities through scavenging activities. He would go out alone or with one other person in search of things to recycle. Bottles and cans were okay, but there was too much competition from other collectors to make it worthwhile. The best find was a newly abandoned car or a newly condemned building. Using a variety of tools, especially crowbars, tire irons, sledgehammers, and large screwdrivers, Jack could remove tires, radiators, batteries, starter motors, seats, and radios from cars. He also became adept at finding and removing copper pipes, brass fixtures, steel sinks, and other items of value from buildings.

Jack wasn't getting rich from this work, but he had managed to save a few dollars. Anyway, he enjoyed the thrill of the hunt, and he began to feel like one of the aboriginal peoples he had read about in high school. They lived off the land and wasted nothing from the animals they killed or the vegetation they cut down. Few Westerners understood their way of life, but he did. Jack now survived using the same code of conduct.

From Communal Living to Shadow Communities

Unfortunately, officials from a state agency called the Department of Real Property came to evict the community in the beginning of January. They stated that residents were illegally occupying a public space and had one week to remove themselves and their possessions. If they failed to do so, a construction crew, with a police escort, would forcibly evict them. These officials placed signs stating their intentions on every structure and quickly made their departure.

Small groups of residents got together immediately to discuss their future. Jack sat with his friend and the guy who lived on the other side of his home, and they each laid out possible courses of action. His friend stated that he intended to stay to the bitter end, chaining himself to his home, if necessary, to keep it from being destroyed. The other guy suggested that they move down the ramp beyond the condemned area and wait for the authorities' next move.

Jack weighed in with a different opinion. He had seen his last home ruined and his possessions destroyed, and he wasn't about to let it happen again. He knew of an abandoned building close by that was not scheduled for demolition until the summer. They could move there for the remainder of the winter and seek an alternative when the weather improved. Jack was convinced he could get the electricity working, maybe even the water.

In the end, no one could convince the others that his plan was best, so they decided to go their own separate ways. Throughout the community, people began to prepare for the attack on their homes and lives. Like Jack, some began the slow process of moving their things from one place to another. Others tried to fortify their homes with additional physical supports to ward off the intruders when they arrived. Still others did nothing, loudly proclaiming to no one in particular that it was all a hoax.

Jack returned to the abandoned building to stake his claim. The structure once had offered ten stories of low-cost or section-eight housing. All entrance-level doors and windows were sealed shut with bricks and mortar. Jack was glad to see the seals remained unbroken, suggesting that drug dealers did not occupy it—yet.

Rather than breaking the seal himself, he decided to climb up onto a ledge on the second floor and enter through a broken window. Once inside, he slid a piece of particleboard across the windowsill so that others would not follow his lead. Jack then began the process of seeking out a safe abode.

After two hours of inspection, he settled on a third-floor apartment that was directly above his new entrance in case he needed to make a quick exit. Jack used the wiring he had brought with him to connect his apartment to the main electrical box on the first floor. He ran the wire along the edge of the flooring, covering its trail with a variety of debris. He then smashed holes in the floors and ceilings to allow the wire to pass between floors.

Over the next several days, Jack moved all of his worldly possessions from his old to his new home. He chose the smallest room among the three in his apartment in which to place his bedding, and he rigged his single light and space heater to operate there. He scavenged several dozen bricks from the first floor and used them to barricade the entrance to his apartment. The only way to enter his home was to scale the wall, a task he hoped would discourage visitors. Jack also removed portions of the hall flooring as well as half the steps in the stairwell between the second and third floors for the same purpose.

He went back to the community one final time to witness its demise. About half the residents remained when the eviction took place, and the scene was like something out of a war film. People scattered as the bulldozers cleared a path through the middle of town, sweeping away their lives in a few short moments. Jack could hear shouting and crying from where he stood, and an hour later there was nothing left but broken dreams and silence.

Not wanting to look upon the destruction any longer, he returned to his new home.

During the succeeding months, Jack spent most of his waking hours scavenging alone for food, clothing, and recyclable items. The apartment building itself was a treasure trove of salable material, from copper wiring to plumbing fixtures to a few stray appliances. Jack increased his grubstake to about a hundred dollars, which he kept hidden in a secret compartment hollowed out of the ceiling above his bedroom.

As the days passed, two other men made their way into the building and established living quarters on the fifth and eighth floors. Jack recognized one as a member of his former community, but the other was a stranger. They never spoke to one another, but they gave each other respectful nods whenever their paths crossed. Jack somehow trusted them, realizing that their survival ultimately was linked in some indeterminate way, at least until it was time to move again.

SUGGESTED READINGS

This chapter was informed by:

Hill, Ronald Paul, and Mark Stamey (1990), "The Homeless in America: An Examination of Possession and Consumption Behaviors," *Journal of Consumer Research* 17 (December), 303–21.

The dramatic growth of homelessness in the last two decades has led to a proliferation of literature on various homeless subpopulations. These works typically fall into two categories: (1) global examinations of the causes and consequences of homelessness; and (2) investigations of living conditions and survival strategies of homeless persons. Examples of both genres are provided below.

Of further interest:

Blau, Joel (1992), *The Visible Poor: Homelessness in the United States*, New York: Oxford University Press. This volume is an excellent example of the first category of text. It provides a compelling rationale for the rise in homelessness experienced during the 1980s and into the 1990s, despite long periods of economic prosperity. Additionally, it describes the causes of homelessness, and estimates the size of the homeless population at approximately 2 million Americans. Finally, its description of current responses to homelessness and elucidation of possible social policy solutions remains relevant as we move into the twenty-first century.

Torrey, E. Fuller (1988), *Nowhere to Go: The Tragic Odyssey of the Homeless Mentally Ill*, New York: Harper & Row. This book is a focused example of the same genre, concentrating on the mentally ill who are living on the streets. While dated, the discussion of the problems associated with survival for seriously mentally ill people who are homeless remains compelling and accurate today. Deinstitutionalization of mental patients without the development of proper community support services is the primary reason for their homelessness. Greater accessibility to public psychiatric services and adequate housing for the seriously mentally ill are recommended as appropriate solutions.

Snow, David A., and Leon Anderson (1993), *Down on Their Luck*, Berkeley: University of California Press. This is the first example of the second category; it chronicles the lives of homeless men and women living in Austin, Texas. An important contribution of this volume is its description of types of homeless people, including the recently dislocated, straddlers, and outsiders. As individuals move from the first to the last type, they increasingly acclimate to and identify with the homeless lifestyle, rejecting the benefits provided by the social welfare system. They also seek shadow work that includes scavenging activities, and they use community to safeguard self and possessions as well as for sharing scarce resources.

Donohue, Timothy E. (1996), *In the Open: Diary of a Homeless Alcoholic*, Chicago: University of Chicago Press. This book chronicles the personal journey of one man into homelessness. Like Jack, the author has experienced a tragic personal life and uses alcohol to blunt his feelings, and he becomes increasingly alienated from mainstream society over time. Additionally, as with Jack, he moves from place to place, experiences the loss of important possessions, and is violated by outsiders. The story is told in the first person, giving the reader a real sense of what it is like to be on the streets. Readers will be astonished to find the author articulate and well educated despite his troubles.

Sheltered Homeless and Homeless Families
Zoë and Her Family Experience Homelessness

Lying, thinking
Last night
How to find my soul a home
Where water is not thirsty
And bread loaf is not stone
I came up with one thing
And I don't believe I'm wrong
That nobody,
But nobody
Can make it out here alone.
　　—Maya Angelou, "Alone"

During the previous decade, the homeless subpopulation became increasingly diverse, with female-headed homeless families one of the fastest-growing segments. By the 1990s, approximately one-third of the homeless were members of family units, and about two-thirds of these persons were children. Many theories have been advanced to explain this rise, but decreases in the stock of affordable housing and increases in the number of poor, single-parent families are the most likely causes.

　　The focus of this chapter is the sheltered homeless and homeless families, who often enter the shelter system after moving through a series of housing situations that are not sustainable. Thus, going from "housed" to "homeless" is rarely a sudden or unexpected event. Instead, it is a process whereby an individual or family moves from a self-sufficient dwelling, such as an apartment, to living with friends or relatives, or in government-controlled, temporary housing, to the streets. After exhausting most or all of these options, many family units seek refuge at a variety of public and private shelters.

The first portion of the chapter examines the process of becoming homeless, and it chronicles a family's move from their own residence to doubling up with extended family or friends to a homeless shelter. The most important explanation for leaving one's own home typically is rent or income factors, while the reason for leaving a doubling-up situation often pertains to stresses associated with living conditions. Unfortunately, once a family is truly homeless, the longer its members are in the shelter system, the less likely they are to leave permanently.

The second portion of the chapter concentrates on life in a private shelter for homeless women and their families which is run by a group of Roman Catholic sisters and a host of volunteers. The women who reside in this shelter cope with their homelessness in a variety of novel ways. First, their detachment from typical consumer goods causes them to place increased value on "sacred" items, such as memories, relationships, and religious beliefs where physical ownership is not relevant, as well as tangible items that are symbolic of these possessions (for example, photographs). Second, a lack of strong bonds between these women and extended family and friends, combined with an inability to support themselves or their families, leads to a childlike reliance upon the sisters and the shelter. Third, fantasies of future home life appear to be a coping mechanism used by the women to deal with the temporary nature of this housing state and their uncertain futures. Sadly, many women fail to move successfully to permanent homes from such shelters and instead remain indefinitely or wander in and out of other temporary residences.

ZOË AND HER FAMILY EXPERIENCE HOMELESSNESS

Childhood Reminiscence

As darkness enveloped the small room housing her family, Zoë allowed the long series of events that had brought her to this shelter in the first place to enter her consciousness. Both of her daughters finally were asleep, exhausted by another search for a place to stay as well as the late hour. Zoë often would reflect after a move of this kind, realizing that it helped her avoid falling into a deep depression.

Her earliest memories were of the good times she had with her parents prior to the birth of her siblings. They did lots of things as a family in those days—picnics, walks in a neighborhood park, and special dinners on holidays. Zoë even remembered when she received her first Barbie doll, and how pleased her parents seemed with her excitement. Unfortunately, their lives changed for the worse over the next several years.

Family problems reached a critical point over a decade ago when she was just ten years old. Her parents had been fighting more often than usual, and Zoë's father stayed home less and less. One day, during a particularly violent argument between her parents, her father began hitting her mother. All three of the children were reduced to tears at this sight, and they begged their father to stop. After a few more minutes, neighbors began banging on the door and threatening to call the police. Her father stopped abruptly and left, and Zoë hadn't seen him since. In fact, he never even returned for his clothing.

The absence of her father transformed their family from a cohesive unit to an assortment of people who went their separate ways. Zoë's mother started staying out late at night with her friends, and she occasionally would allow strange men to sleep in her bedroom. This erratic and irresponsible behavior made Zoë furious at first, but she learned to keep her feelings to herself. As long as she had her bedroom door locked and her siblings inside, she felt some degree of comfort and safety from her mother's escapades.

The mornings after such indiscretions were usually the same. The kids got up by themselves, turned on the television, and searched the kitchen for food. If they were lucky, a box of cereal was available, and they covered the sugar-coated grains with Kool-Aide since fresh milk rarely was available in their house. Other times they had to make do with some leftover pizza or fast food; sometimes there was nothing at all. On occasion the woman who lived next door invited them over for a hot meal, the culinary highlight of their young lives.

Over time the mother started leaving the children alone for several days at a stretch, with Zoë as guardian. The responsibility for her siblings' care left Zoë anxious and confused. What could she possibly do to improve their situation? Food was scarce, bill collectors called day and night, and the electricity recently had been turned off. Zoë felt helpless and abandoned.

As her mother's absences increased in duration, Zoë spent more time at home and less time in school. Her teachers noticed changes in her attendance as well as in her deportment, and they contacted the state board for child welfare. A caseworker was sent to investigate the situation, and she knocked on their front door one weekday morning. After a few minutes of stilted conversation, she convinced Zoë to let her into the apartment.

At first Zoë cried silently and refused to answer the caseworker's questions. However, with the tears came a sense of relief. For the first time since her father left home, Zoë was able to express her feelings. In her heart she knew that something was wrong with her mother and that an adult needed to do something to help them.

As the caseworker walked through the apartment, she began writing in a small notebook. Occasionally she would ask questions: When was the last time you saw your mother? Who is responsible for making your meals? For bathing you or your siblings? During her evaluation, the caseworker found virtually no food, little clean clothing for the children, poor hygienic conditions, and an absence of adult supervision.

In the end she decided to remove the children and place them in a temporary foster home. Zoë and her siblings were taken to a holding area for several hours as they waited for three beds to become available. At about 7:00 that evening, each child was placed in a different establishment, separating them for the first time in their lives. Zoë cried herself to sleep that night, and she refused to go to school for an entire week. She later realized that she had experienced the first of many bouts with depression.

Over the succeeding months, the children moved from one foster home to another, and they were together only once for about a week. Zoë did get to see her mother on a few occasions. She looked older and sadder than Zoë remembered her. She told Zoë that her problems had caught up with her, and that she would have to go away for a while. Looking back on these events from an adult perspective, Zoë came to understand that her mother was addicted to crack cocaine.

Zoë and her siblings stayed in the foster care system for the next several years until their mother finally found the courage to give up drugs. She got herself a steady job and rented a small apartment in their old neighborhood. After she demonstrated six months of employment and a full year without drugs, the state finally agreed to let her children return home.

Unfortunately, it was too late for Zoë. She was now fourteen years old, almost a full-grown woman. Her initial anxieties had matured into anger and depression, and she was uninterested in listening to her mother's warnings or commands. The siblings she had supervised in what seemed like another life were virtually strangers, raised by different people from across town. Zoë quickly fell in with a fast crowd at school, experimenting with drugs and sex to alleviate her emotional pain. She attended classes sporadically, and her moods alternated between manic highs and desperate lows.

Living with Family and Friends

When Zoë was seventeen, she became pregnant with her first child. The father was probably one of two men she had regularly been intimate with over the course of the previous year. However, neither was a part of her life anymore, and she was uninterested in sharing her child with either of them. She considered abortion briefly, but decided in the end that having a child might help alleviate the sense of loneliness and the depression that had haunted her since she and her siblings were taken from their mother.

Her experience of pregnancy was uneventful, except for the changes in her body. Zoë erratically took the vitamins prescribed by a physician at the local city hospital, and she avoided contact with the public health nurse assigned to her case through the state's medical program for the poor. As time passed and the date of the birth of her child drew near, Zoë became increasingly anxious and withdrawn.

Her daughter was born in early December, about a week after the Thanksgiving Day celebration. She was underweight at four and one-half pounds, but she was healthy in all other respects. Zoë was glad she had stopped using drugs and alcohol after she discovered she was pregnant, one of the few pieces of advice from her physician that she had explicitly followed.

She spent only twenty-four hours in the hospital, just enough time to catch her breath after delivery. Her siblings and her mother made a great fuss over the baby during the first few days after Zoë's return home, but they tired of the baby's late-night crying and other disruptions before long. Suddenly their small apartment seemed even smaller. The baby slept in the same bed as Zoë, sharing the tiny bedroom with her brother and sister. The only other rooms were a bathroom, a modest kitchen, and a living area with a television. Whenever she gave comfort to her colicky child in these shared quarters, someone would complain and she and her daughter would be banished to the bedroom.

When spring finally arrived, Zoë's mood brightened considerably. She could now take the baby outside for long walks, and this opportunity to escape the confines of the apartment gave her renewed energy. Even the baby acted up less, and they both enjoyed the attention they received from neighbors and other passersby. On these walks, she sometimes would chat with old friends, and they would talk about their lives at school, their boyfriends, or upcoming parties. Zoë felt left out of these events, and she began to resent her responsibilities as a mother.

One evening, several of her girlfriends stopped by to visit on their way to a local dance club. As they were about to leave, Zoë asked them to wait for a moment. She ran into her mother's bedroom and begged her mother to watch her daughter for a few hours so she could go out with them. Zoë promised she wouldn't ask again anytime soon. Her mother looked at her sympathetically but frowned, seeing much of herself in her daughter for the first time. In the end, her mother let her go but admonished her to avoid drifting back into her previous lifestyle.

Zoë had one of the best times in her life at the club, dancing, smoking, and drinking until dawn. When she arrived home, groggy and hungover, her mother greeted her at the door with her daughter in hand. It was 5:00 A.M., her child was up for the day, and her mother needed to get ready for work. Regardless of Zoë's physical condition, the baby was her responsibility.

This experience was transformational for Zoë. She saw in herself that part of her mother that needed to self-medicate her emotional pain away after the breakup of her marriage. Zoë knew she wasn't addicted to drugs, but she sure enjoyed the party life. However, her primary obligation was to her daughter, and she vowed to keep her own consumption in check as she looked down into the eyes of her child.

One positive outcome of that evening for Zoë was that she met a man whose company she enjoyed. He was twenty-five years old, seven years her senior. He had his own apartment in a nearby neighborhood and a steady job in a local factory. Over the next several months he visited her often, and Zoë and her daughter spent several weekends at his place so that they could have some privacy. He played with her daughter constantly, and Zoë began to fantasize that he was the father and that they were one big happy family.

Six months later, Zoë discovered she was pregnant again. She told her mother immediately, expecting her mother to be excited about the birth of a true love child. However, her mother reacted angrily, telling Zoë in no uncertain terms that there was no room in their overcrowded apartment for another baby. Besides, she could no longer afford to pay for the extra food and clothing as well as the diapers and other baby products Zoë's children would need.

At first Zoë was disheartened by this response, but her new man greeted her news with an altogether different reaction. He was excited about the birth of the child, and he invited Zoë and her daughter to move in with him while they waited for the baby to be born. His place was even smaller than her mother's was, so they decided to turn his mini-living room into a nursery. Their home would be cramped for a while, but they planned to move to larger accommodations after he received his next raise and promotion to supervisor.

Zoë religiously followed all of her doctor's instructions, and she avoided drugs, alcohol, and cigarettes. As a result, her second daughter was born at exactly nine months, a seven-pound, eight-ounce beauty. Taking the baby home to the man she loved was like a fairy tale to Zoë, a dream she believed only others could live. They even talked about marriage in a year or two, when they could afford to have a big wedding.

Sadly, things did not go as planned. Her man never received the promotion; instead, he was reduced to part-time status due to a slowdown of activity at the factory. He now earned about two-thirds of his previous income, and they were barely able to pay their bills. A few months later the landlord informed them that the building had been sold to developers who planned to renovate the units and sell them as condominiums. They would have three months in which to decide either to purchase their home or to vacate the premises. Given their current financial situation, they were forced to leave.

Their most immediate concern was where to go next. With two young children, their options were not very broad. Few apartment buildings in their community had two-bedroom units that they could afford on his part-time salary. Additionally, most of their family and friends already lived in close quarters, as Zoë's mother was quick to point out. In the end they decided to split up, with Zoë and the girls moving in with his mother, and her man rooming with a friend.

Zoë packed up what clothing and toys she could carry in a single suitcase, and she stored the remainder of their possessions in the crawlspace above her grandmother's bedroom. Her man placed his work clothing, casual clothes, and toiletries in a large laundry bag and took them to the efficiency apartment he would share with his buddy. They said a tearful goodbye before they went their separate ways, and they vowed to be together each evening.

When Zoë arrived at his mother's home, she felt an immediate chill in the air. Zoë had met her on a few occasions, and she always felt the woman disapproved of her. She adored her son, as many mothers do, and she felt Zoë wasn't good enough for him. While she did seem to appreciate her only granddaughter from a distance, she was not very interested in caring for her.

They each settled into their new homes during the next several weeks, and they were able to reunite almost daily. They rarely had any privacy since they both shared rooms—her man with his friend, and Zoë and the girls with his younger sister. When they were together, they tried to forget their present circumstances, and they regularly talked about their hopes for the future.

One evening, after a long night spent trying to get her daughters to fall asleep, Zoë's living circumstances took another turn for the worse. Her man's uncle, who visited the house regularly following his drinking binges at a local bar, crept into her shared bedroom one evening. The children and Zoë's roommate were resting peacefully as he settled into bed next to her. He began touching Zoë in a feeble attempt to start a romantic interlude, and she responded by going rigid and begging him to leave. As his moves became increasingly aggressive and her refusals more pronounced, one of her daughters awoke and began to cry. His mood was broken by this interruption, and he quickly left the room.

The next morning Zoë went to her man's mother and described the night's events. Surprisingly, the mother defended her brother's actions by telling Zoë that she must have seduced him, as she had her son. Zoë was angered by this characterization, and she refused to stay there another minute. She gathered up her children, packed their meager belongings, and called for a cab.

Once the cab arrived and they were all settled in, the issue of her destination became a problem. Where could she go? Her own mother had no space for them, her man had no additional room where he was lodging, and she had little money for rent. In desperation, she decided to go to her maternal grandmother's house. This woman had agreed to store their possessions; maybe she would let them live in her den for a while.

When they arrived at her grandmother's doorstep, the woman was just finishing her morning coffee. She was a rather distant person who had battled her own demons all her life. No one in her family had ever come to her for long-term support in the past, including when her own daughter (Zoë's mother) was institutionalized. To Zoë's relief, her grandmother listened to her troubles and agreed to let her stay the night. However, Zoë and the girls would have to leave the next morning. The place was just too small to accommodate four people.

Seeking Shelter

In the morning Zoë fed her daughters a light breakfast from the items available in her grandmother's cupboard. It wasn't much, but it was the best she could do under the circumstances. She spoke on the telephone with her man at his workplace, and they decided she had no choice but to call the city's family services and find emergency housing. Following this decision Zoë felt her emotions darken with the onset of another depression, but she did everything in her power to bury these feelings for the sake of her children.

A machine answered the phone when she contacted the housing authority, and it instructed the caller to report to a facility downtown for placement. She dressed her daughters in warm clothing, packed up her remaining possessions, and called for a cab. As she waited on the front steps for her ride to arrive, Zoë counted her remaining money. Her grandmother had given her an additional five dollars, and she now had a total of $12.50. After the cab ride, she knew that her nest egg would be reduced to a few dollars and some change.

The travel time from her grandmother's home to the housing authority building was about twenty minutes, and the fare was $9.75. Embarrassed by her inability to afford much of a tip, Zoë hurriedly shoved two five-dollar bills at the cabby, scooped up her two daughters in one arm, and grabbed her suitcase. As she entered the front door, she immediately was bombarded by a dozen laminated signs, each pointing in a different direction. Zoë became increasingly disconcerted and agitated by this information overload, and she decided to go to the help desk on the second floor.

The line of people at the desk was eight deep, and she heard at least three different languages being spoken. The woman at the front of the line was screaming at the worker behind the counter, and he nodded in her general direction with a look of indifference on his face. It was forty-five minutes before Zoë was served, and she was quickly dismissed and sent to the fourth floor.

On the fourth floor she obediently took her place behind six other women at the intake window. To Zoë's relief, this line moved more rapidly than the last one, but she was disappointed to find that its only purpose was to provide a call number for a screening interview. Although she might have to wait up to four hours before someone was available, she was told not to leave the room. If she missed her interview, she would have to start the process all over again. Zoë and her children took a seat on the hard wooden benches in the back of the room and settled in for the duration.

After about two hours, Zoë's back ached and her children were hungry. She searched through her possessions for something to eat, and she discovered a plastic bag containing some Cheerios that she had packed at her grandmother's house. As her children dined on their small piles of cereal, Zoë ran out of the room and over to a vending machine. She deposited her remaining two dollars and received two eight-ounce cartons of whole milk in return. She hoped this now rare treat would quiet her daughters for the rest of their wait.

Almost exactly four hours after their arrival, Zoë was called to an interview. Both of her girls were asleep, exhausted by their journey. She was hesitant to leave them alone on the bench, so she gathered them up in her arms as carefully as possible in an attempt to avoid waking them. They stirred and clung to her shoulders as she hurried into the adjoining room, pushing her suitcase along with her feet.

The interviewer was a short stocky woman with a no-nonsense look about her. She asked Zoë a number of questions and expected her to give short, crisp responses. Most were rather simple, but Zoë was unable to provide some of the necessary answers and forms of identification. The woman told her that she could place her family in a cross-town shelter for the night, but that they would have to return tomorrow if they wished to stay another night or find a more permanent residence. When Zoë explained that she had no more money for carfare, the woman passed her several bus tokens for the round-trip.

By the time she boarded the bus, Zoë was livid. She had spent over five hours at that office, most of it waiting. All she had to show for her trouble were two cranky children, some bus tokens, and a stay in one of the worst sections of town. Zoë wanted to scream at the top of her lungs and run away from her problems. Instead, she swallowed her emotions and turned her attention to her daughters in preparation for their hour-long ride.

Shelter Living

When they first arrived at the facility, Zoë and her children stood on the sidewalk, staring at the front door. She imagined it was filled with the worst possible people, including the kind of bums and bag ladies she had passed on the streets over the years. Nonetheless, it was getting colder outside as the day progressed, and Zoë realized she had no choice but to go inside.

Mustering all her courage, Zoë picked up her daughters and suitcase and climbed the front steps. She opened the front door and stared down a long hallway that led to a large cavernous room containing the living quarters. The placard at the entrance advised new guests to register at the main office located inside and to the left. Zoë was relieved to find no one in line ahead of her at the help window, but she waited almost ten minutes anyway before someone came forward to assist her.

The woman who waited on her seemed angry about being disturbed, and Zoë was almost apologetic with her requests. She told the woman that she had nowhere else to go, and that she had been referred to the shelter by family services. The woman made a nodding motion that signaled neither agreement nor concern as she seated herself at a computer terminal. She then interrupted Zoë with a series of questions that seemed unrelated to her family's current situation. Zoë answered them dutifully, however, fearful that the woman might otherwise refuse her lodging.

Zoë was assigned living area number forty-five, and she was handed sheets and blankets for two beds, three pillows and some towels, a small tube of toothpaste, and a toothbrush for personal hygiene. The woman told her that the facility was not responsible for the loss of her possessions, and that Zoë should keep them with her at all times. Zoë's mind wandered to a scene in which she was bathing her children in a shower stall with their suitcase somehow in attendance. How could that possibly work?

When the woman finished her instructions, Zoë asked if there was any food at the facility for her daughters. The woman told her that food and drink were prohibited in the living quarters, but that there were many fast-food restaurants near the facility which accepted city meal coupons. She then passed Zoë $12.00 in scrip—$5.00 for herself and $3.50 for each of her daughters.

With her family and cargo in tow, Zoë walked down the hallway to the living quarters in search of number forty-five. As she entered the room, its size and the level of commotion caught her by surprise. There were ten rows of enclosed areas that were at least five deep. Sheer blankets that moved with the rhythm of activity nearby separated each area. It was clear to Zoë that this feeble attempt to create some privacy did not succeed. However, she was reassured by the fact that no male over the age of ten was allowed to stay past 8:00 P.M.

It took Zoë several minutes to locate her dwelling since the ordering of the living areas was not readily apparent. She noted immediately that all four shelters surrounding her abode were occupied, and she began to feel claustrophobic. Zoë quickly made the two beds using the sheets and blankets provided. Both were lumpy and worn, and the sheets themselves were threadbare in several places. When this task was completed, she changed the clothing of both daughters and removed the money and identification papers from her suitcase.

Her next step was clear. There was no way she could lug everything she owned with her to the restaurant and back. So, she would have to do her best to place her possessions and the items provided by the facility out of harm's way. Zoë shoved the suitcase under one of the beds, and she arranged the towels and toiletries under the other. In order to conceal them further, she pulled the blankets down over the sides of the bed as far as possible. When she was satisfied that she had done all she could to safeguard her things, she picked up her daughters and headed out for their meal.

The temperature outside was dropping rapidly, and Zoë calculated that the girls would become uncomfortable quickly. She looked down both sides of the city block and headed for the closest restaurant, which was a McDonald's. While she knew that the food wasn't particularly nutritious, it would be filling and the restaurant would be clean. Besides, they could stay as long as they liked without bothering anybody.

Once inside she quickly ordered two boxes of animal crackers and two cartons of whole milk for her daughters, and a Super-Value meal composed of a double-cheeseburger, large fries, and a

Coke for herself. All of a sudden Zoë realized that she hadn't eaten since early morning and that she was famished. They consumed their food quickly, as if someone might take it away at any moment. Zoë decided to top off her meal with some coffee for herself and some ice cream for the girls, and she went to the counter to place her order. She walked back to their table with these items a few moments later and sipped her coffee as she carefully spooned the frozen treat into her daughters' mouths. After an hour or so had passed, Zoë grabbed the girls, one in each arm, and reluctantly started back to their new home.

By the time they reached the shelter, they had approximately thirty minutes before lights out. Zoë marched over to number forty-five in search of her towels and toiletries so that she could prepare herself and her daughters for bed. Once inside her dwelling, she saw immediately that things were not as she had left them. The pillows and blankets were gone, and two of the three towels were missing. Her suitcase lay open between the two beds, and most of the clothing and toys had been removed.

Zoë ran out of the room and down the hallway to report this theft to the authorities. She went to the same help window and beckoned to the same woman who had waited on her previously. Zoë told the woman about the missing items and how much they meant to her family. The woman coldly acknowledged the likelihood of her loss and reminded Zoë to keep her possessions with her at all times. Zoë became increasingly agitated by this response, and she asked how this was possible during her trek for food with two children in tow. The woman shrugged her shoulders in disgust and said it was not her problem.

Feeling defeated, Zoë slowly walked back to number forty-five, gathered up the remaining towel and toiletries, and headed for the bathroom. She carefully wiped down each girl using warm water and gentle strokes. When both were cleaned to the best of her ability, Zoë brushed her own teeth, washed her face, and combed her hair.

They returned to their dwelling, and Zoë took the sheet off her bed to use as a covering for her daughters. She was tucking them into bed as the lights began to dim, and she quickly kissed them goodnight and spoke in a gentle voice as they drifted toward sleep. Zoë then took what clothes remained in her suitcase and used them to cover the soiled mattress on her bed. She lay down for the first time that day, physically exhausted but mentally alert. She prayed silently that the occasional outcry from other children or their mothers would not awaken her daughters, and that their luck would change in the morning.

The lights were turned on at 6:00 A.M., but Zoë was already awake. One of her girls had been startled during the night, and Zoë moved this daughter into bed with her to avoid disturbing the other. That had been at 4:30 A.M., and Zoë hadn't slept a wink since that time. She spent the next hour and a half wondering what to do next.

Unclear about her next move, Zoë waited in line with the other women to obtain more food coupons. Her load was considerably lighter without the missing items in her suitcase, a small consolation. When it was her turn at the window, Zoë was given the same twelve dollars in scrip that she had received the previous evening.

She arrived at McDonald's ten minutes later and ordered more animal crackers and some apple juice for her daughters, and an Egg McMuffin and coffee for herself. They feasted heartily on these foodstuffs, savoring every bite. After they were finished, Zoë went to a pay phone and called her man at his friend's house.

He answered on the first ring as if he was expecting the call. Her man was delighted to hear her voice, and he had spent the previous night tossing and turning in his makeshift bed, consumed with worry. Zoë calmed him by explaining that she and the girls were fine; she decided not to tell him about their mishaps. However, she did inform him that there was no way they could return for another night. The cross-town trip to receive permission for another stay was too grueling to imagine, and Zoë didn't think the girls would be able to sleep peacefully a second time.

Her man excitedly told her about a private shelter he had located that was within walking distance of his new home. It was run by a group of Catholic nuns who provided donated clothing and food to residents, as well as a private room that they could occupy for up to a month. By that time, her man predicted he would have enough money to afford a two-bedroom apartment. Once again, he would not be able to stay with them, but he could visit each evening. He would borrow a car from a co-worker to transport them to their new home, and he would get them within the hour.

As Zoë waited for him to arrive, she pondered this turn of events. It certainly seemed better than any alternative, and the thought of seeing her man brightened her mood. The idea of a private room, for the first time in recent memory, also increased her sense of well-being.

When he arrived at the restaurant, Zoë and her children were waiting in the parking lot. They embraced for a long while, and tears rolled down Zoë's cheeks. Once they were together in the car, she allowed herself to tell him everything that had happened during the previous twenty-four hours. Her man listened sympathetically, and he reassured her that things were about to improve.

The shelter was located at the corner of a busy intersection in a lower-class suburb just outside the city limits. Across the street was a Gothic-style Catholic church that provided some financial support for the shelter. The small sign on the front door noted that the Sisters of Mercy, an international group of nuns and volunteers who served the poor, ran the facility.

The shelter was closed to the public until 4:00 P.M., at which time residents were welcome to return. Since that was almost seven hours away, they decided to spend the rest of the day together. They went to the zoo, ate lunch at a family-style restaurant, and window-shopped at many of the stores in a local mall. Zoë fantasized that their troubles were over and that they were a normal middle-class family enjoying a day of leisure.

Their reverie was disrupted when her man noticed that it was nearly 3:00 P.M. They would have to hurry back to the shelter and wait in line for a room. After the short ride, he parked the car and helped her carry the suitcase and the children to a spot behind four other families. They hugged and promised to see each other the next evening.

The doors opened at exactly 4:00 P.M., and a cheerful woman emerged beckoning the first three families to enter. Zoë was filled with anxiety that her family might be sent away, along with the others in line with her. Fortunately, the same woman returned fifteen minutes later, and she invited Zoë's family and two others to come inside.

As they entered the facility, they were gently ushered into a private room across from the dining area. Zoë approached the table cautiously, frightened by the small woman dressed in black-and-white religious clothing behind the desk. She spoke in broken English, but her message was clear—she was not here to judge Zoë's past but to help her in the present. As long as Zoë followed the rules of conduct, she and her children would be allowed to stay for up to one month. Unsure of what these rules entailed, Zoë agreed to them anyway, relieved to have a more permanent home.

The Meaning of Possessions

After reminiscing about her family's road to homelessness, Zoë drifted off to sleep for the first time in her new home. She dreamed that the woman from the city shelter chased her up and down the rows of covered dwellings, and that the sheer blankets that provided a modicum of privacy whipped up as they sped past, exposing the inhabitants. Zoë realized in all this commotion that her daughters were missing, and she scanned each living area in search of them. She awoke in panic several times during the night, and she reached over to make sure her children were safe before settling back down in her bed.

Over the next several weeks, their family established a comforting routine. Zoë and her children ate breakfast and dinner at the shelter, and they spent their days in a variety of places, including the library, a fast-food restaurant, a local community center, and a strip mall. Her man visited almost every evening, and he regularly gave her a few dollars from his weekly paycheck.

As time passed, Zoë learned several things about living at the shelter. For example, as she watched the sisters and volunteers prepare the meals, she was surprised at how they managed the food stock. The shelter received tons of foodstuffs donated by a variety of groceries, bakeries, and food banks throughout the city. In fact, the shelter had so much of some items that they spoiled before they could be eaten. Nonetheless, the sisters always prepared meals using the oldest produce first, as if throwing away a piece of moldy bread might result in someone's starving to death. Zoë assumed that this procedure had something to do with their religious background.

Each meal followed a prescribed pattern, opening with a group prayer. The women, their children, the volunteers, and the nuns stood at attention while looking at a picture of Jesus Christ and recited the words out loud. The residents would then sit, and the volunteers would serve the food. Seconds were rare since the sisters were adept at preparing just enough to fill their plates. When the meal was over, they cleared their own tables and swept the dining area. After breakfast Zoë and her children were required to leave the facility until 4:00 P.M. Following dinner they usually met with her man for an hour's visit.

The other shared accommodations at the shelter had their own routines. After dinner most of the women and their children retired to the community room located on the second floor. It contained an old television set that ran continuously, a bookshelf filled with tattered magazines such as *Glamour, Time,* and *People,* as well as some novels and religious pamphlets, and several couches and chairs that lined the perimeter. The children typically ran up and down the room as the women smoked cigarettes, complained about their current misfortunes, and discussed their plans for the future.

Following this free time, each family was assigned a half-hour period for their private use of the shared bathrooms. During this interval, family members would bathe or shower, brush their teeth, use the toilet, and do whatever else they needed to do before retiring to bed. Zoë found it impossible to accomplish all of these tasks for herself as well as her daughters in the time allotted, and she regularly was driven from the room before she was finished.

Their sleeping quarters were rather barren, containing just two single beds, a chest of drawers, and a crucifix that hung on the wall. The mattresses were old but in fair condition, and the sheets, blankets, and pillows were a step above those available in the municipal shelter. At night Zoë could hear conversations from other rooms through the thin walls, but she was relieved to have private quarters and a safe place for her remaining things.

Clothing, toiletries, and toys for her children were another matter altogether. Individuals as well as civic groups and churches from the more affluent surrounding communities regularly brought donated property to the shelter. The nuns stored these goods in a one-room house behind the facility, and the women were allowed to go in and select items for their personal use once a week. Most objects were in good condition, even if they were a bit outdated. Zoë had plenty of shirts, pants, and jackets that fit her family well enough. However, shoes, socks, and underwear were hard to come by. Because of this situation, most of the women discarded clothes rather than wash them, and they replaced them weekly with new (used) items. The few hard-to-find products received better treatment.

Zoë was surprised at how the women reacted to the shelter's rules, regulations, and routines. Several of the women reverted to childlike behaviors, with the nuns and the volunteers acting in the role of parent. Some in this group reminded her of young children who needed to be scolded when they violated the rules or praised when they followed them. Others acted like rebellious teenagers, always searching for ways to subvert authority, for example, by bringing alcohol into the shelter or sneaking out to visit boyfriends. Zoë didn't know why they acted in these ways, but she felt it might have something to do with the lack of strong parental figures in their lives.

Zoë belonged to a second group of women who believed that the philosophy of care at the shelter represented an unnecessary intrusion into their adult lives. They felt that they were capable of making their own decisions about what to eat, when to bathe, and how to spend their free time without comment or direction from others. While they appreciated the helping hand, they were frustrated at the inflexibility of the rules and the arbitrary nature in which they were enforced. If they or their children were sick, why couldn't they spend the day in bed? If they were hungry at 10:00 P.M., why couldn't they go to the kitchen and eat some of the excess produce?

During this period Zoë began to clarify her own relationship with material possessions. Food, clothing, and a stable living arrangement held new meaning for her. Zoë now realized that she had spent much of her life searching for some constancy in the availability of these things, and her decision to get pregnant and her choice of men were driven by the same concerns. Now that these basic commodities were available to her without question, her anxieties subsided and she was able to appreciate their functionality without exaggerating their importance to her survival.

This detachment from consumer goods allowed her to recognize what was truly important in her life. She began to value more highly the bond between her and her daughters and the love between her and her man. Items that reminded her of the good times she experienced as a young woman, such as a small gift from her father and photographs of her family of origin before he left home, became her most prized possessions, and she kept them with her everywhere she went. Zoë promised herself that she would remember this lesson no matter what the future held for her.

Coping with the Future

Nonetheless, Zoë's equilibrium was thrown out of balance on occasion when other women left the shelter permanently. A few departed of their own accord, having resolved the problems that resulted in their homelessness in the first place. Most women, however, either returned to unsatisfactory previous lives within a month or were forced to live on the streets because of some infraction of the rules. For example, Zoë knew of two mothers who returned to their abusive spouses at the end of their stay. They honestly believed they had no reasonable alternative. Three others had broken the rules by coming to the shelter either stoned or drunk, and they were expelled immediately.

When these events occurred, Zoë calmed herself by daydreaming about a future home. In these reveries, Zoë, her daughters, and her man lived as she and her parents had during their best times. They occupied a pleasant two-bedroom apartment that overlooked a community playground. They ate meals together as a family, and Zoë was able to stay home with her children and attend to their needs. In the evenings they would take long walks in the park; on weekends they would picnic on the lawn in front of their building. Although money was tight, they were able to afford the things they really needed. Their apartment was sparsely furnished, but it contained several framed pictures of them taken on special occasions such as Christmas or birthdays. The bedrooms were their private sanctuaries, allowing the girls as well as Zoë to have a secure and protected place to escape the external world. Her man received his long overdue promotion to supervisor, and they planned to marry and move into their own row house next year.

Unfortunately, after six weeks at the shelter Zoë was asked to leave to make room for another family. Zoë was told that she was almost two weeks beyond the one-month time limit and that other needy families were waiting their turn for shelter. Zoë pleaded that she had no place else to go. Her man had been laid off from his factory job a week ago, and he was forced to move back home with his mother. She had called all of her adult relatives, and none was able to come to her aid.

The sisters were sympathetic but firm. Since they were unfamiliar with the social welfare system outside their own private facility, they asked one of the male volunteers to intercede on Zoë's behalf. This person was a white male from an educated background, and the sisters felt that he would command more respect from the bureaucrats in the housing section of family services. He called their emergency shelter number and began explaining Zoë's situation to the gatekeepers on the other end of the phone.

Zoë listened as he argued with several different parties, his frustration level rising quickly. She took this as a negative sign, and her own emotions began to well up inside her. Zoë was paralyzed with fear for herself as well as for her daughters. Tears began to flow, and she was unable to provide comfort to her children. Two other volunteers picked them up and tried to entertain them. The girls stopped crying, but they refused to be engaged, going into their own protective worlds.

Zoë could feel herself slipping away, helpless to do anything about it. Random events, thoughts, and ideas entered and left her head, and she began to see bright lights before her eyes. At some point the volunteer hung up the phone and began giving her advice. He seemed to be very far away, and his words came to her as a soft whisper. Zoë was confused and unsure how to react, so she continued looking straight ahead as if he was a fading memory.

SUGGESTED READINGS

This chapter was informed by:

Wasson, Renya Reed, and Ronald Paul Hill (1998), "The Process of Becoming Homeless: An Investigation of Female-Headed Families Living in Poverty," *Journal of Consumer Affairs* 32 (Winter), 320–42.

Hill, Ronald Paul (1991), "Homeless Women, Special Possessions, and the Meaning of 'Home': An Ethnographic Case Study," *Journal of Consumer Research* 18 (December), 298–310.

Of further interest:

Golden, Stephanie (1992), *The Women Outside: Meanings and Myths of Homelessness*, Berkeley: University of California Press. This book parallels the research used to inform the second portion of the chapter. The author chronicles her work during the late 1970s and early 1980s at a shelter for homeless women sponsored by a group of Roman Catholic nuns. The shelter is described as a permanent community that took on the qualities of a family, with the sisters and volunteers occupying caretaker roles. This homelike environment allowed the residents to rescue their collective sense of self despite their overwhelmingly negative circumstances and the vagaries of street life. Fantasies among the domiciled population about homeless women, which are in contrast to their true lived experiences, also are presented.

Kozol, Jonathan (1988), *Rachel and Her Children: Homeless Families in America*, New York: Crown Publishers. In this volume the author examines the trials and tribulations of the sheltered homeless, with a special focus on homeless families in New York City. The words of the author's informants make their dire living conditions come to life for the reader. Their living quarters in city shelters, for example, are described as dangerous to body and soul. Many residents feel imprisoned within the shelter and the social welfare systems, unable to improve their circumstances but fearful of ending up on the streets worse off than they currently are. As Rachel herself suggests, the greatest fear often is for their children—the loss of their innocence and, potentially, their futures.

Nunez, Ralph daCosta (1994), *Hopes, Dreams & Promise: The Future of Homeless Children in America*, New York: Institute for Children and Poverty. Although the title may suggest otherwise, this book focuses attention on family homelessness. The author interweaves personal vignettes with secondary data and policy solutions to describe and provide answers to this "new American poverty." The primary causes of family homelessness are the political policies of the Reagan administration which resulted in crippling cuts in social programs for the poor. While state and local efforts have attempted to make up the difference, they have been unable to do more than supply emergency shelter and basic commodities. An alternative to the traditional shelter system is provided through a discussion of a residential educational training center model. This approach concentrates on family preservation programs along with adult and family education. The long-term goal for homeless families is independent living in permanent housing.

Seltser, Barry Jay, and Donald E. Miller (1993), *Homeless Families: The Struggle for Dignity*, Urbana: University of Illinois Press. Like two of the previously cited volumes, this book uses the voices and experiences of the homeless themselves to give the reader an understanding of their situation. For example, the authors use these data to examine the impact of the welfare and shelter systems on the feelings and sense of dignity of homeless families. Additionally, coping mechanisms of homeless parents are described, with an emphasis on the various defense mechanisms used to maintain their self-esteem. The book closes with a series of moral reflections as well as a discussion of broader cultural values as they relate to homeless persons.

FOUR

Poor Children and Juvenile Delinquency
Fast Eddie Comes of Age

Little boy, who left you
to wander alone
in this hard city,
in these fearsome streets?

Little boy, who scarred you
with fire, with fist,
with words hurled like knives
into your fragile spirit?

Little boy, who now will take your hand
and shout your cause
and hear your pain
and lead you home?
—Debra Lynn Stephens, "Little Boy."

Throughout the 1990s, approximately 20 percent of American children lived in poverty, totaling nearly 14 million boys and girls at any one point in time. These children faced discontinuity and deprivation in access to basic necessities, including food, clothing, housing, education, and health care. Combined with higher rates of family disintegration caused by divorce, desertion, and abuse, these hardships often resulted in developmental delays, depression and anxiety, and low self-esteem among poor children.

The focus of this chapter is the impact of poverty on children, and it chronicles the journey of one such individual from birth until his eighteenth year. Several dislocations such as movement in and out of welfare hotels and section-eight (public) housing projects, as well as a sporadic and violent relationship with his father, mar his early childhood. He copes with these uncertainties through fantasies about lost and desired possessions and through strong relationships with his peers.

Over time, the innocent glow of childhood is extinguished as the realities of an impoverished life come into focus. Like all children his age, this one sees the vivid media portrayals of middle-class family life, along with sumptuous foods, toys and games, and other possessions too numerous to mention. He looks at his own life and meager belongings in comparison and finds that he fails to measure up. Each birthday is a disappointment; Christmas and the fantasy of Santa Claus are a sham. His daily life seems to reinforce his low status, wreaking havoc on his self-esteem.

Childish dreams eventually are replaced during adolescence with anger at society and a determination to have the good life before it is too late. Some of the adults in his community have conventional lives, raising their children as best they can and working at traditional jobs. However, many of these people eventually are able to leave, choosing more affluent and safer neighborhoods. Those who remain barely survive by living on welfare or working at low-paying service jobs. The few successful ones, those who are truly able to live the material life extolled by advertisers, often engage in criminal activities such as drug dealing or fencing stolen merchandise.

This young man believes his choices, like those of millions of others in similar circumstances, are clear. He can work hard to attain a second-class education at the rundown school in his community, most likely ending up in a minimum-wage job. Alternatively, he can join others in his peer group and live for today, not tomorrow. They may sell drugs, steal cars, or commit other property crimes in order to have immediate access to automobiles, clothes, and other expensive items. From his perspective, why not? With the level of violence in his neighborhood, he might die tonight no matter what he does.

However, the good life eventually comes crashing down when he is arrested, and he learns to live by a more socially acceptable set of rules in a private facility for juvenile felons. The high school equivalency diploma he receives during his stay, as well as other forms of positive reinforcement, bolsters his commitment to reform. Will it last when he returns to his old neighborhood and faces his peer group and previous living environment?

FAST EDDIE COMES OF AGE

Eddie Goes Down

As the police officer handcuffed his wrists, Fast Eddie realized that he had stolen one too many cars and now must pay the price. His mom looked over at him with great sadness in her eyes while his friends tried to bolster him with an occasional remark about how he's still the man. This turn of events led Eddie to experience the fear that he no longer controlled his own life, as if he were a child, but he kept this feeling to himself in order to avoid worrying his mom or losing face in front of his pals.

Fast Eddie then was escorted to a waiting police van that would take him to the detention facility. His two escorts moved quickly to secure Eddie in the back seat as his entourage pleaded with them to let Eddie go free. They drove off without making eye contact with the small band of supporters, and Fast Eddie settled in for the one-hour ride.

As he passed through the familiar streets of his neighborhood, he remembered that today was his seventeenth birthday. He fantasized about what it would be like if he were home tonight. The alcohol would flow, the drugs would be plentiful, and the girls would be trying to get next to him. Instead, he had to resign himself to this lost opportunity to party. As he began to sing the traditional birthday song in a low whisper, Fast Eddie vowed that he would be back on the streets living the good life before too long.

Nonetheless, his anxiety level continued to rise as the van passed through familiar city neighborhoods and into the suburbs. Fast Eddie gazed out the window in awe of the large homes, ornate lawns, and expensive cars in the driveways. He knew how those people got them—they were born lucky. He also knew what he had to do in order to have similar possessions.

The suburbs eventually gave way to the open spaces characteristic of rural areas. After driving an additional ten minutes, the van turned off the main road into a dirt driveway beside a sign identifying the area as a national park. Fast Eddie looked around at the openness in mild panic. He felt almost naked out here without his streets, their buildings, and the friends who populated them. This primitive feeling unleashed a stream of recollections from his earliest years.

From Birth to Kindergarten

Fast Eddie was born when his mother was barely fourteen years old. During the first few years of his life, they lived together at his grandmother's place, a three-bedroom row house in the northern section of the city. After Eddie's brother and sister were born, his grandmother asked them to leave. She told them that there just wasn't enough room for their entire family in her tiny home.

His grandmother took them to the welfare office, and she showed Eddie's mom how to complete all the paperwork necessary to receive a benefit check. Eddie's mom was terrified at the prospect of living on her own, and she was certain that she would receive little support from the father of her children. Once all the forms were filled out properly and their identification was verified, their family was assigned to a welfare hotel until permanent housing could be found. When his mother asked how long that might be, she was told that the typical wait was approximately two years.

They went back to his grandmother's house to collect their things for their move into the welfare hotel. The four of them would occupy a small, one-bedroom unit on the south side, far away from their family and friends. His mother collected what clothing and other necessities she could pack into two suitcases, and she told Eddie to select one toy to bring with him. He cried at this command and did his best to explain the impossibility of choosing among his most cherished possessions. However, she was adamant that he could bring only one thing since it was possible that they would move several times over the next two years as they waited for subsidized housing to become available. She told him there just wasn't enough room for all his possessions, and they would have to be prepared to pack and leave on a moment's notice.

Some of Eddie's most vivid and powerful memories are of life in that first hotel. As they exited the subway on their way to their new home, they found themselves in a part of town his mother did not recognize. They walked several blocks until they came upon a tall building with trash piled six feet high on the sidewalk out front. Two men sat on the steps leading to the front door sharing a bottle of wine.

The two elevators in the hotel were out of order, so his mother had to carry his brother and sister as well as their larger suitcase up the stairs to the third floor. Eddie walked behind them hauling their smaller bag and his Teenage Mutant Ninja Turtle toy along with him. When they arrived at the door, they could hear a woman and a man fighting loudly in the room next door. Their harsh words and obvious anger frightened Eddie, and he clung to his mother's leg until they were safely inside their own apartment.

The interior of their new home was drab and sparsely furnished. Paint was peeling off the walls and ceilings, and the carpets were stained and worn in several places. The bedroom contained two single beds, one for his mother and the other for his sister. Eddie and his brother would share the dilapidated pull-out couch in the living room. As that first day progressed into night and darkness descended upon them, Eddie worried that their noisy neighbors might break through the flimsy walls and harm them. His mother assured him that nothing of the sort could happen, but he stayed alert most of the night just in case.

Over the next several months, the family settled into an unnatural routine. They rarely left the building unless they needed food or additional supplies, and their only other contact with the outside world was a small black-and-white television that survived their move. No one visited them at their new home, including his father. Eddie remembered the embarrassing habit he developed in that tension-filled time of wetting his bed at night.

They moved every couple of months during the next few years, never completely acclimating to any particular residence. On a few occasions social workers stopped by to check on them, and his mother answered their questions without providing a realistic picture of their lives. This confused Eddie, and he asked her why she had lied to these women. His mother told him that they were not to be trusted, and that if she were more honest with them, the women might take away their home.

This new information haunted Eddie during this difficult period, and he began to feel anxious and out of control. He now hid in the bedroom every time someone knocked on their door, refusing to come out until they left. Increasingly he spent his free time daydreaming about having his own room so that he could escape possible eviction. His fantasy abode had a steel door that was impenetrable without his permission, and the room contained great quantities of the possessions he had left behind because of his moves. Sometimes Eddie would fantasize that he was a rich kid capable of summoning everything his family needed instantaneously.

Almost exactly three years after they began their search for a new dwelling, the city office of housing services placed them in a permanent home. They were assigned apartment number 845 in one of the low-rent, high-rise buildings on the south side of the city. It was a two-bedroom unit with a small kitchen and living area. Eddie's mother was nervous about the neighborhood, especially the drugs and the resulting violence, but he was excited that they would not be moving around anymore.

To Eddie's surprise, his father joined them in their new home, sleeping with his mother for the first time in his memory. At first Eddie was happy to have another adult around, relieved that he would no longer be asked to do so much for his family. However, after the initial euphoria wore off, his father stopped having any interaction with them except when he was angry. He drank heavily most evenings and yelled at or slapped the children if they disturbed him. Eddie learned to tiptoe around him and to speak to him only when addressed directly.

His Early School Years

When the van carrying Fast Eddie came to a stop in front of the detention facility, his reverie about the past abruptly ended. He craned his neck to see the exterior facade of the building, and he noticed a large sign identifying the site as Saint Peter's Home for Boys. Eddie recalled the judge's offer: he could go to a lock-down juvenile detention center in the middle of the state or attend school fifty miles from his home at Saint Peter's. Fast Eddie didn't spend much time considering his options. Everybody in his neighborhood knew that Saint Pete's was a better deal. He might even receive his high school diploma while in residence.

The two police officers walked him through the front doors and into the first office on the left. A woman looked up from her computer screen as soon as they entered and told them that an intake counselor would be available in a few moments. She took a file from one of the officers and placed it with other materials that had Eddie's name written on them. For some reason this pile of written information made Eddie feel very paranoid, but he refused to let his feelings show. If he could survive being around his father as a child, he could endure detention at Saint Pete's.

After several minutes, a portly man who looked like an aging hippie entered the room. He exchanged a few words with the officers, and they removed the handcuffs from Fast Eddie's wrists. He began rubbing them in order to get rid of the numbness, and he waited for directions from this new authority figure. As the police strolled out the door, the man invited Eddie into an adjoining room. Fast Eddie followed his order without acknowledging the man's existence.

When they entered the room, the man sat down behind a large wooden desk, and he invited Eddie to sit in the seat in front of him. Fast Eddie maintained his most nonchalant facial expression as he slumped down in the chair. The man examined the material on Eddie that had caused his earlier discomfort, and he began reciting facts about Eddie's early schooling in order to place him in the appropriate classes at Saint Pete's. Once again, Fast Eddie's mind drifted to earlier times.

Eddie entered school at the age of six, terrified to be separated from his mother and siblings. While some of his school-age peers had attended the Head Start program in his community, the majority was in the classroom for the first time. Because of this situation, his teachers expended much effort trying to acclimate these novices to classroom etiquette.

Eddie was shy and reserved during his early years, but his work was well above average and he began receiving praise from his instructors. He eventually met a male teacher who took a particular interest in him, working with him after school on special projects for more advanced students. Eddie remembered this attention with both pride and embarrassment. While it made him feel good about himself, he knew that some of his peers looked upon him and other high achievers with contempt.

After school Eddie often would go home and sit in front of the television set with his siblings to watch their favorite programs. They enjoyed a variety of cartoon shows as well as situation comedies that portrayed family life. He particularly liked sitcoms such as *The Cosby Show* and *Family Ties*, and his favorite episodes involved holiday events and birthdays. Meals were lovingly prepared, and there was always an abundance of his favorite foods. Families exchanged gifts, and Santa Claus visited each year, bringing special presents for everyone.

Eddie liked the advertisements as much as the shows themselves, especially during the time between Thanksgiving and Christmas. While the programs portrayed the importance of family during the holidays, the commercials demonstrated that the real meaning was in material goods. An endless parade of toys, games, clothes, videos, and other items too numerous to mention danced before his eyes, and he looked at them in eager anticipation. He was fully aware that they were available to good girls and boys, and Eddie felt entitled to his fair share.

Unfortunately, Eddie never experienced holidays the way the TV families did. His father typically began drinking soon after breakfast on these special days, and he was either asleep or in a drunken stupor by dinnertime. Church groups from more affluent communities donated most of the food they consumed at these meals, consisting of a variety of canned and packaged meats, vegetables, and starches. The food wasn't bad, but it certainly did not live up to Eddie's fantasies of an old-fashioned holiday feast.

Gift giving at Christmas was even more disappointing. Eddie would make lengthy lists of desired items that he had seen on television, and he would send them to Santa Claus for delivery. During the best of times he would receive one of the smaller toys he had requested, or some piece of clothing that his mother felt he needed such as socks or shoes. One year he got nothing at all, and his father laughingly handed him a dollar bill and told him to keep the change.

Birthdays followed a similar routine. There were no parties— no guests, no balloons, no presents, and no games. Birthday cakes, if they existed at all, were store-bought cupcakes complemented by a small scoop of ice cream. On his tenth birthday Eddie's mother tried to do something extraordinary, but his father spoiled the event by eating the special treat his mother had prepared an hour before Eddie's best friend from school arrived.

His self-esteem also was damaged through comparisons with his peers in the community. Because of his family's income level, Eddie was eligible for a free lunch at school. However, he was required to stand in a special line to receive this meal, and he was forced to sit at a particular table with other poor children. Eddie was certain that the rest of the kids at school knew their situation, and the obvious association humiliated him. As a result, he never looked up from his food and left the table as soon as possible.

Clothing and school supplies held similar difficulties for Eddie. Most of his wardrobe came from secondhand stores or from charitable organizations. They neither fit exactly right nor represented the newest styles. Even his friends teased him about being out of touch with the latest fashions. Additionally, he often went to school without the required pencils, paper, or other materials, and his teachers looked at him as if he personally had done something wrong. Eddie pleaded with his mother to buy him new clothing and school supplies, but she told him that there wasn't enough money to purchase their day-to-day necessities, much less those items.

Over time Eddie began to experience a kind of emotional deadening with regard to material possessions. He lost his enthusiasm for the holidays and other special occasions, and his birthday became just another day. Santa Claus didn't exist for him anymore, and the display of material goods in television commercials only elicited apathy from him. Even his favorite programs provided little relief from the realities of his life. They represented a fantasy world that didn't exist in his universe.

His family was another matter. While his mother tried to keep them going, his father did everything he could to disrupt their lives. He came and went as he pleased, and he was verbally and physically abusive to them all. His father was particularly challenging toward Eddie. He regularly taunted Eddie, and he slapped Eddie around whenever he was drinking. Eddie became increasingly withdrawn in his father's presence, retreating to his shared bedroom whenever his father was home. Eddie stayed outside with his friends as much as possible, and they became his primary support in these turbulent surroundings.

His Teen Years

Fast Eddie snapped back into the present when the intake counselor began asking him a series of questions. Eddie looked up at him and responded to each query with just a word or two. These brief remarks only led to more probing questions, which Eddie countered with similarly short answers. Eddie could have been more elaborate in his replies, but his life was his own business and no one else's.

By the time Eddie became a teenager, his father had permanently left the family home. He was living with a woman on the other side of town, and it was rumored that he had fathered another child. From Eddie's perspective it was good riddance. The man had cast a dark shadow on their lives, and their home was a better place in his absence. Over the course of the next several years, Eddie ran into him only once but avoided making eye contact to ensure that no real association was made. He hoped that the next time he saw his father would be at the man's funeral.

While his father had been rough and mean, his mother remained gentle and submissive. She let the children do whatever they wanted in their father's absence, allowing them to attend school as they pleased and stay outside with their friends until late into the evening. As Eddie matured he took full advantage of these freedoms, wandering the neighborhood with his friends until three or four in the morning and sleeping until noon. At best he went to school for a few hours each day, and he typically missed all of his morning classes. Most of his close friends followed a similar routine.

Eddie grew up fast spending so much time on the streets. His first sexual experience occurred when he was only thirteen years old. He was with a large group of teens, and one of the older boys had dared his partner to have sex with him. She was a sexually active older teen who thought Eddie was cute, and she was eager to introduce a young virgin to intercourse. Since that time he had been with too many girls to remember the total number, much less their names. As a result, Eddie was convinced that he had never been in love. Sex was something to take from a woman, and he enjoyed the erotic pleasure of it as often as possible.

The streets also introduced Eddie to a violent landscape. His neighborhood lacked swimming pools, recreation centers, playgrounds, and movie theaters. However, it did contain drug houses, cheap motels, porn shops, and liquor stores. Except for the occasional basketball game, Eddie and his friends hung out and spent their time getting stoned on pot or drinking malt liquor. Under the influence of these substances, they often would seek out teens from other neighborhoods for fights. Most of the time they used their fists, but as they aged, the members of Eddie's gang resorted to knives and blunt instruments such as baseball bats and crowbars in order to inflict more damage.

Eddie knew of three kids who had suffered serious injuries during these fights, one of whom eventually died. In that particular incident, his gang had been attacked as they were returning home from playing basketball at one of the local schools. They had taken a short-cut through a city block that was known for its gang-related activities. Halfway down the street they were challenged by some teens for trespassing on their turf. They had no choice but to defend themselves. The fight was pretty even until someone pulled out a gun and shot Eddie's buddy in the chest. He died two days later in a local public hospital.

In this brutal existence, Fast Eddie learned to rely first and foremost on his friends for survival. They did everything together, enjoying as sensual a life as possible. On occasion, they would vandalize or destroy property to demonstrate their anger at society and to exert control over their neighborhood. Most of them had graffiti tags that they sprayed on the sides of buildings, buses, and cars late at night. Together, they were invincible. Apart, they were nothing.

Fast Eddie's role models were the older teens in his community who seemed to have it all. They had access to illegal drugs, expensive cars, fashionable clothes, and beautiful girls, and everybody in their neighborhood knew who they were and of their affluence. They flaunted their ability to buy material things, and they spread the wealth around among their peers. For example, they might buy beer and sandwiches for all of their friends on a hot afternoon, or take a trip to the mall on a weekend to buy matching clothes for everybody. The source of their income was clear—they engaged in some form of criminal activity such as selling drugs or fencing stolen merchandise.

Attending classes at school was a useless exercise that held no meaning for them beyond the social connections. Eddie realized that the kids who studied hard and got good grades ended up in low-paying jobs anyway, and they were just as likely to be shot on the streets and robbed as the drug dealers. While the rare exception might go to college, he or she would be forced to leave the neighborhood. Eddie realized he could never abandon his friends, even if he had the ability and income to attend such an institution.

Fast Eddie decided that following the rules was for suckers who failed to understand how things really worked. As a result, he stopped going to school altogether when he was challenged beyond his ability to absorb classroom material without much effort. School just wasn't worth his time since it was unlikely to help him improve his standard of living. Fast Eddie would have to make money by illicit means if he wanted to enjoy the good things in life. For example, some of his friends had begun stealing cars and selling them for cash. They showed Eddie how he could make the equivalent of a month's salary at a fast-food restaurant like McDonald's with only an hour's effort. Additionally, he would have the use of the car of his dreams before exchanging it for money. The material possessions he had always wanted were now within his grasp, and he was eager finally to have them.

Living la Vida Loca

When the interview was over, the counselor walked Eddie from the main administrative building over to the dormitory where all the residents lived. Eddie was not eligible to reside in one of the fraternities on the second or third floor until his teachers and the dormitory staff could gauge his maturity level through observation of his behavior. He was expected to live in the sleeping area on the ground floor for approximately one week before being admitted to a frat.

Eddie was assigned a bunk and a storage area for his possessions by the prefect on the floor. As he stowed his clothing and other things away, he noticed that four of the nearby bunks had occupants. These teens looked as if they could be from Eddie's neighborhood, and this familiarity comforted him.

About an hour later, they were ushered out by the prefect and into one of three dining areas in the dorm. Fast Eddie followed the others to an empty table and sat silently waiting for his food. One of the servers brought him a plate without comment, and Eddie wolfed the food down as if he hadn't eaten for days. The food was a bit bland, but it was better than he had anticipated.

When the meal was finished, Fast Eddie and the rest of his dorm mates returned to their living area for some rest and relaxation. They were not allowed to smoke, but they could watch television or play pool as long as they behaved. He listened to the sounds coming from the TV and decided that the program was not worthy of his attention. Instead, Eddie decided to lie on his bed and reminisce about better times.

Fast Eddie vividly recalled the thrilling aspects of his life prior to incarceration. He and his friends became like hunters in a concrete jungle, fully engaged in the moment and taking what they wanted to gain control over their lives. They would use the spoils of their conquests to get access to material goods that they would never have been able to afford otherwise. Eddie also knew that the money made them popular with the girls. He could feel his adrenaline level rising just thinking about it.

The routine was rather simple. They would take the bus in the evenings from their neighborhood to the mall on the outskirts of the city. The bus stopped right in front of the main parking tower, one of their primary hunting grounds. They typically would go up to the higher levels, feeling more secure in less-traveled areas. Eddie searched for red sports cars of any make. They were his signature automobiles, and everybody in his neighborhood recognized him when he drove by in one.

After they spotted their target, one or two of his friends would stand watch while Eddie broke into the car. Fast Eddie could break into any automobile and disarm its alarm or remove the steering wheel guard in less than thirty seconds. In fact, that is how he got his nickname. He would use a long metal instrument to reach inside the door panel and deactivate the lock. Then he would remove a device such as the Club by sawing through the steering wheel with a hacksaw and pulling it out from the top. Two minutes later he would have the ignition system hot-wired and the car started.

Once they were safely away from the mall, Fast Eddie and his friends would rummage through the glove box, trunk, and any other compartments in the car where items typically are stored. They never knew what they might find. Over the last year or so Eddie had acquired an assortment of drugs, jewelry, firearms, clothing, and sports equipment, as well as a significant amount of cash.

The next step involved taking the car back to their neighborhood and showing it off to their friends. They took turns driving it up and down the streets, running the engine at top speed and making the tires screech as they drove past the houses of girls they were trying to impress. They continued similar abuses most of the night, doing whatever they pleased to the car without any regard for its condition. In fact, a few times they made a game out of seeing how much damage they could do to a car while keeping it running.

After they became bored or physically exhausted, they took what remained of the car to a garage a few blocks from their neighborhood. This facility was the drop for stolen cars that were fenced by a local businessman who operated a used car lot and parts supply house about two miles away. When Eddie first met the dealer's representative at the garage, the man tried to cheat him by telling Eddie that his car was too old, too conspicuous, or too foreign to be unloaded profitably. Under these circumstances he could afford to give Eddie only $1,500 for a car that Eddie knew was worth more than $30,000. Unfortunately, Eddie's need to unload the car was greater than the man's desire for additional supply, so Eddie grudgingly accepted the deal. Over time and after they began to trust each other, the payoff increased to $2,000.

The day after these escapades, Eddie liked to walk the streets of his neighborhood with a big wad of bills in his pocket, sharing his wealth. One time he bought five of his buddies cheese-steak sandwiches and forty-ounce bottles of beer for lunch. Another time he took the same group and their girls out to the movies, paying for the show as well as all the refreshments they could consume. The money typically was spent quickly, lasting no more than a few days. Fast Eddie didn't mind because he was rapidly becoming a big man in his community. Even the younger boys in his neighborhood started to look up to him.

After a while, stealing cars became almost an obsession with Fast Eddie, consuming most of his waking hours. Without access to expensive cars, there would be no spending money, no good-looking girls, no liquor to drink, and no stylish clothes. However, most of the sites where cars were plentiful, especially the local mall, were receiving increased surveillance from the police and security guards as a result of his efforts. Even Fast Eddie wasn't fast enough to get into a car and out of the parking lot in time under these new conditions. The last few car thefts had led to high-speed pursuit by the cops, and he and his friends had been forced to abandon two of these cars and take flight before they could do anything with them. Eddie began to feel paranoid and worried that he might finally get caught.

In order to improve his chances of finding the right car without complications, Fast Eddie and two of his friends decided to avoid the mall as well as other prime locations that now received increased attention from the authorities. Instead, they drove to an affluent city neighborhood a few miles away, and they cruised up and down its several blocks looking for Eddie's automobile of choice. Most of the expensive cars were safely tucked away in garages, out of their view and reach. However, just before they were ready to give up and head back home, one of his buddies spied a bright red Mustang convertible parked in the driveway of a large, well-lighted home.

Eddie was conflicted about what to do next. He wanted that car—he *had* to have it. Nonetheless, it was going to be a difficult job. Clearly someone was inside the house, most likely the owner. Any noise or unwelcome strangers surely would attract attention and lead to a call to the local police station. However, Eddie decided to go for it anyway. He was out of money and needed to replenish his supply.

The driver parked their car halfway down the street in front of a small wooded area. He stayed in the car with the engine running, ready to make a quick getaway if things went wrong. Fast Eddie got out of the car and walked slowly toward the Mustang. His other friend placed himself on the corner of the property opposite the driveway and within sight of the front door. It was his job to signal Eddie if someone from the house came outside.

Fast Eddie slid down along the driver's side of the car to avoid easy detection from any of the windows facing the street. He opened the door of the Mustang easily, with a sly grin at this skillful maneuver. He could feel the thrill of the hunt rising within him, and his heart began pounding. However, as he slithered into the automobile, an alarm began emitting an urgent tone, and Eddie scrambled around in the front seat trying to find a way to disarm it. Eddie realized that he had tripped a motion detector of some kind, one that he had not confronted previously.

For a split second Fast Eddie considered abandoning his quest and running back to the getaway car. Instead he summoned all his courage and became more determined than ever to capture his prey. He quickly locked the car doors and began dismantling the ignition. He heard his buddy signaling the approach of someone from the house, and he tried to speed up his movements. The Mustang started up as the owner attempted to enter the car from outside. Ten seconds later Fast Eddie was roaring down the street in his new Ford, with the previous owner in pursuit on foot.

As Eddie rounded the corner three blocks away, he slowed down and started to feel his whole body relax. He had known this sensation many times before, and it reminded him of the feeling he experienced following sexual intercourse. In fact, the act of stealing a car had a lot in common with sex, including anticipation, climax, and relief.

He headed back to his neighborhood, ready to follow his usual routine. He picked up his two accomplices, and they drove around their community talking to friends, smoking pot, and drinking malt liquor. Fast Eddie dropped them off at their homes around 2:00 A.M., and he headed for the garage in search of his reward.

As he approached the facility, he noticed that there were no cars parked out in front and the lights were turned off. Fast Eddie was surprised since the garage had never been closed previously. He drove past the front entrance several times before deciding it was unsafe to stop. However, as he made his departure, a police car pulled in behind him, flashing its blue and red lights.

Fast Eddie knew he could not pull over, but he feigned compliance by slowing down and edging toward the curb. When he was convinced the police believed his intent was to stop, he jammed the gas pedal to the floor and took off as fast as the car would go. The police hesitated only a moment and then gave chase. Eddie was certain he could lose them if he could get back to his own turf. He knew those streets better than anyone did, and he could outrun most cars in his new Mustang.

As he sped along, taking corners nearly at top speed, he realized that the cops were aware of the garage's activities. If he was lucky enough to get away this time, he would have nowhere to go to fence the car. Maybe he would be better off ditching the Ford and trying to run through his neighborhood on foot, eventually backtracking to the safety of his own home.

As Eddie entered more familiar streets with the police still in pursuit, he decided to drive the car into a chain-link fence that surrounded a small tavern. When his Ford rammed into the front gate, Eddie leaped out the door on the driver's side and scaled the fence. He ran at top speed, vaulted the back of the fence, and fell into the waiting arms of two other policemen. They threw him facedown on the concrete sidewalk. One of the officers slapped handcuffs shut on his wrists as the other began reading him his rights.

A Transformational Experience

Fast Eddie's first few weeks at Saint Peter's were very difficult for him. He had lived by his own rules ever since his father abandoned their family, and having to conform to all the regulations at Saint Pete's was disconcerting. For the first time in years, Eddie was required to rise, dress, shower, eat, urinate, study, relax, and sleep on command.

His labor began at 6:30 in the morning every day except Sunday. His entire floor showered at the same time in a facility that was reminiscent of a high school locker room, and the lack of privacy bothered Eddie. Breakfast followed personal hygiene on their schedule, and they marched silently in single file into the dining area to their assigned tables. No one ever criticized the food because negative comments resulted in kitchen duty for a minimum of one week.

After breakfast they were ushered into the classrooms, and their first class began promptly at 8:00 A.M. Schoolwork continued until noon, with an hour for lunch and recess. They resumed working at exactly 1:00 P.M. and persisted until 4:00 P.M. Those interested in organized sports then joined their teams for practice for the next two hours. All others were required to go to study hall and read quietly until dinnertime.

Dinner was served at 6:00, following the same routine as all other meals. Plates of food were brought to the teens for their consumption, and they were required to move all dishes, utensils, and waste to the appropriate containers when they finished. At 7:00 P.M. they were allowed to retire to their living areas and engage in a variety of officially sanctioned activities such as reading, playing billiards or Ping-Pong, watching TV, or card playing. At 9:30 P.M. they were ushered back into the shared bathroom to brush their teeth, urinate, and otherwise prepare themselves for sleep. Lights were turned off at precisely 10:00 P.M.

The campus itself was as disconcerting as the rules and regulations. Fast Eddie felt as if he were living in an underground cave, typically moving from building to building through enclosed walkways without venturing outside. However, the few times when he was able to leave the immediate property, Eddie experienced a sense of panic at the expansiveness of the state park that surrounded the facility. He had spent his entire life in the city and had never visited any mountains, beaches, parks, or forests that gave him the opportunity to see for miles. It seemed unnatural and unsafe to be so out in the open. He felt like a sitting duck waiting to be picked off by a hunter.

Eddie also felt stripped of the material goods he had worked so hard to accumulate during the past several years. He was allowed to keep only a few changes of clothing and two or three pairs of shoes in his storage area, along with a small number of other possessions. Most of his wardrobe that had set him apart as somebody in his neighborhood stayed behind with his family. His gold jewelry and expensive watches also were left at home, and carrying money was not allowed. He had no stereo and CDs, no television and cable channels, and no VCR and movies. Of course, store-bought foods, liquor, and illegal drugs were prohibited.

Like many others during the early days of their incarceration, Eddie rebelled against the system on a few occasions. He refused to get out of bed one morning and was caught smoking in a restricted area once. For these minor infractions, he was ordered to perform some of the most onerous tasks available as punishment such as cleaning the toilets. If he refused, he would be shipped out of Saint Peter's and taken to an even more rigid detention facility. Thus, to avoid expulsion Eddie did what he was told, and he eventually began obeying the rules as closely as possible.

Some of the teens, however, didn't fare as well. A small group with acute impulse-control problems engaged in acts that were deemed intolerable by the administration. For example, a few masturbated publicly, unable to manage their sexual urges while away from females. Others smuggled drugs into the dorms and were caught dispensing them to their peers. Still others tried to escape by fleeing into the surrounding woods, usually finding themselves hopelessly lost and unable to locate their neighborhoods. Most of these youths were sent away and never returned to Saint Peter's.

Once Fast Eddie was admitted to a fraternity on the third floor, his primary outlet for rebellion was through his personal bulletin board. These panels were the only unrestricted space in the entire facility, and Eddie was allowed to do anything with his board that he pleased. Most of these boards contained pictures of items representing the teens' previous lives, including photographs and small posters of girls, cars, guns, and drugs. Fast Eddie's board was much the same—a tribute to the status that he had attained in his neighborhood through criminal activities.

Without his friends, possessions, and the familiarity of his neighborhood, Eddie began to feel cast adrift. He no longer had his prior identity, living in a sea of other teens in the same situation. However, over time he began to appreciate the order and security of daily life at Saint Pete's, as well as its profound impact upon his sense of self. For the first time in recent memory Eddie was receiving good grades, and he could honestly say that he enjoyed learning. One of his teachers urged him to take the high school equivalency exam after six months of schooling, and he passed all sections on the first try.

With this initial success bolstering his sense of self, Eddie slowly began to realize that he might have a future beyond a life of crime. He talked regularly to the counselors at the school about trade programs that he might attend after leaving Saint Peter's, and he even considered enrolling in one of the local community colleges to pursue computer training. If none of these options materialized, Eddie thought he could take his newly minted diploma to one of the clothing stores in the mall and gain employment as a salesperson. He smiled at the thought of going back to the scene of many crimes to do legitimate work.

Even his bulletin board evolved over time. Most of the pictures of guns and cars were gone. In their place he prominently displayed his academic honors from school, his notification of passing the equivalency exam, and advertisements for trade schools. As he looked around, he noticed that most of the teens who successfully survived to the end of their time at Saint Peter's had made similar transitions.

After spending a full year at Saint Peter's, Eddie was brought before a judge and officially released from his incarceration. He was placed on probation for two years and was required to meet with a probation officer once every two weeks during that period. When the judge asked Eddie what his plans for the future were, he proudly described several alternatives for career training or employment. Eddie told him in no uncertain terms that his criminal activities were behind him. The only car he wanted to drive was one he purchased himself with his own paycheck.

As he packed his meager belongings and said goodbye to the members of his fraternity, he took a look around at the place that

had become his home. He had changed a lot in a year, but the uncertainties associated with his next step left him anxious. It was
easy to be committed to change on the inside, but would his resolve last on the outside? He was going back home to live in the
same place in the same neighborhood. He had nowhere else to
go. How would his old friends treat him? Did the opportunities
he had discussed with the counselors at Saint Peter's really exist?

Eddie Goes Home

When Eddie knocked on the front door of his family home a few
hours later, his mother answered the door with tears in her eyes.
While she had visited him regularly over the course of his incarceration, she worried about his physical safety among all those
troubled youths. Eddie couldn't help chuckling at her belief that
he was somehow safer on the streets of his neighborhood just because she had daily contact with him.

His mother announced that she had planned a big eighteenth
birthday party for him that evening, and that she had invited all of
his closest friends. The thought of being around his old gang excited and frightened him at the same time. It would be great to
see his buddies again, enjoying their camaraderie and the status
he had attained over the years among them. However, he wasn't
the Fast Eddie anymore whom they had admired. Would they
notice the change? Would they accept him anyway?

Eddie's fears melted away when the party began and his
friends joined the festivities one or two at a time, greeting him
with affectionate hugs and high-fives. He recounted some of his
best stories about life at Saint Peter's, and his audience howled
with laughter or shook their heads in disgust depending upon the
appropriate response. Occasionally someone would shout that
Fast Eddie was back, and he turned in the direction of the voice
and flashed a wide smile. However, in the back of his mind he was
beginning to experience turmoil. If he had truly changed, how
could the old Fast Eddie return?

During the next two weeks, Eddie only left the apartment twice—to meet with his probation officer and to accompany his mother to the supermarket. The rest of the time he was either combing the employment section of the paper looking for work, or calling trade schools to get admission information. His friends dropped by regularly, especially in the evenings when they were looking for some excitement. Eddie pretended that he was still exhausted from the shift in his routine, and he told them that he would catch up with them later. Eventually they took the hint and stopped coming by at all.

As the days passed, his initial euphoria about his future prospects evaporated and was replaced with a sense of dark resignation. Most of the schools he had hoped to attend were beyond his financial reach, and his ability to secure a loan to cover tuition and expenses was severely constrained because of his felony conviction. The managers of the clothing stores in the mall almost laughed at his equivalency diploma, treating him like an educational second-class citizen. The few who were desperate enough to give him an application withdrew their offers when his background check identified him as a convicted car thief.

Eddie felt that he was at one of the lowest points in his life. After all his work at Saint Peter's he was no better off than he was before he left the neighborhood. Eddie was unable to move forward—none of the options he had fantasized about during the latter part of his detention were viable alternatives. He also was uncomfortable going backward—living his previous life would most likely result in real jail time that would make his prior incarceration look like a picnic.

After living in this limbo state for a while, Eddie drifted back to the streets, seeking comfort by re-establishing relationships with the friends he had recently abandoned. Without money he was seriously constrained in what he could do, and he was dependent upon the successful criminals in his neighborhood, who had taken his place while he was away, for their benevolence. He hoped he could avoid returning to a life of crime, but what else could he do? There was nowhere left to turn.

SUGGESTED READINGS

This chapter was informed by:

Hill, Ronald Paul (1992), "Criminal Receiving: The Fence as Marketer," *Journal of Public Policy and Marketing* 11 (Fall), 126–34.

———— (1992), "Homeless Children: Coping with Material Losses," *Journal of Consumer Affairs* 26 (Winter), 274–87.

Ozanne, Julie L., Ronald Paul Hill, and Newell D. Wright (1998), "Juvenile Delinquents' Use of Consumption as Cultural Resistance: Implications for Juvenile Reform Programs and Public Policy," *Journal of Public Policy and Marketing* 17 (Fall), 185–96.

Of further interest:

Chase-Lansdale, P. Lindsay, and Jeanne Brooks-Gunn (1995), *Escape from Poverty: What Makes a Difference for Children?* Cambridge: Cambridge University Press. This edited text opens with some startling numbers. Nearly one-third of all children live below the poverty line sometime between birth and age fifteen, and almost a quarter of very young children (three years of age or less) live in poverty. The statistics are even worse for people of color. For example, 24 percent of African-American children live under conditions of poverty for at least ten years, and approximately 60 percent of African-American and Hispanic single-mother families are poor. The editors take a broad and dynamic approach to defining poverty, and include factors beyond income such as material resources and community services. To this end, individual chapters explore ways to deal with the deleterious effects of poverty on children through changes in maternal employment, child care, father involvement, and access to health care. This volume closes with policy recommendations and ideas for future research initiatives.

Mayer, Susan E. (1997), *What Money Can't Buy: Family Income and Children's Life Chances*, Cambridge: Harvard University Press. The author of this book shares the widely held belief that poor children differ significantly from their more affluent counterparts. They weigh less at birth, are more likely to die in their first year of life, and score lower on standardized tests. They also are more likely to drop out of school, have children during their teen years, and get into trouble with the law. Some social scientists claim that these problems stem entirely from a lack of income to meet basic material needs. As the author puts it, the underlying belief is that "the poor are just like everyone else except that they have less money." However, through an extensive evaluation of extant research, she demonstrates that increasing parents' income improves children's material standard of living, but it has little influence on the other variables mentioned. Instead, parental characteristics associated with their poverty are more likely to affect their children's well-being and adjustment to adult life.

Maynard, Rebecca A. (1997), *Kids Having Kids: Economic Costs and Social Consequences of Teen Pregnancy*, Washington, D.C.: The Urban Institute Press. This edited volume contains individual chapters by some of the most respected scholars in the fields of economics and poverty studies. Important findings include the following: Children born to teen mothers average lower cognitive achievement scores regardless of their socioeconomic status. These children also tend to be in poorer health than children born to older mothers. They are more likely to suffer from abuse and neglect, and they are more likely to end up incarcerated. Early fatherhood is associated with less schooling, lower income, and fewer hours worked in the job market. Delaying childbearing until age twenty would save taxpayers between $6 billion and $9 billion annually. The policy implications are clearly explicated and relevant to the discussion in this chapter.

Parent, Marc (1996), *Turning Stones: My Days and Nights with Children at Risk*, New York: Harcourt Brace & Company. This volume chronicles the life and times of the author in his job as a caseworker in New York City's Emergency Children's Services. The first seven chapters provide a vivid portrait of the lives of abused children, describing their suffering as well as their bravery in the face of circumstances that are largely beyond their control. Not all of these youngsters live in poverty, but the conditions described by the author are more likely to exist within impoverished communities. While the book lacks explicit policy directions, Parent's sympathetic look at the children, combined with his realistic view of the department empowered to help them, makes an important political statement.

Welfare Mothers and Their Families

Anita, the Welfare Mother

I finally understand
For a woman it ain't easy tryin' to raise a man
You always was committed
A poor single mother on welfare, tell me how ya did it
There's no way I can pay you back
But the plan is to show you that I understand
You are appreciated.

— 2Pac, "Dear Mama"

The closing decade of the twentieth century ushered in sweeping reform proposals for the welfare safety net in the United States. Introduced originally by President Franklin Roosevelt as a response to the Great Depression, this system of support became the primary vehicle for the provision of basic consumer goods and services to almost 5 million impoverished families by the mid-1990s. Reform proposals were crafted according to the historic guiding principles of decreased dependency and personal responsibility. To this end, legislation from both Republicans and Democrats concentrated on reducing benefits, requiring work, and capping total welfare spending regardless of need.

During the debates on these reforms, politicians characterized children as innocent victims of the welfare system, whose lives were trapped in poverty as a result of their parents' dependence on financial and material support from the government.

Consistent with this perspective, welfare parents were viewed as incapable or irresponsible caregivers, lacking the ability or desire to support their own progeny independently. Finally, the welfare system itself was seen as a corrupter of societal values which sought to destroy the family by reducing the likelihood of marriage and promoting single parenthood.

An important concern voiced during this debate was the extent to which the discussion was informed by the experiences of people who actually subsist within the welfare system. Research suggests that welfare families endure significant constraints on their ability to meet basic consumption needs when compared with more affluent consumers. For example, their ability to buy or afford products is restricted, and the availability of goods and services within their communities is limited. The consequences of these restrictions are decidedly negative, and responses take the form of emotional reactions such as anger, humiliation, alienation, and feelings of loss of control. Nonetheless, welfare mothers must find ways to cope with this negativity, including behavioral approaches that are operationalized as budgeting or saving, under-the-table work, and external financial support, and emotional approaches such as distancing from other welfare recipients, fantasies about the future, and external emotional support.

Taken together, these perspectives suggest that the welfare system prior to reform failed to operate properly as a consumer safety net from the perspectives of both constituencies. However, while the political debate focused on the corruption of values due to dependence on government handouts, welfare families found the provision of income, goods, and services deficient, and this lack was a source of great emotional distress. Thus, the political conclusion of *too much* is out of balance with the welfare families' lived experience of *too little*.

ANITA, THE WELFARE MOTHER

The Road to Welfare

Anita grew up in a small row house in a poor suburban area south of the city. She lived in this home with her grandmother, mother, and four siblings. These quarters were cramped and lacked privacy, with several persons sharing each bedroom and everyone using the only bathroom. Anita had few items of clothing or playthings, and she was forced to go to bed hungry on several occasions. Twice during her early life the electricity was turned off, and she vividly remembers shivering all night long underneath the pile of blankets and clothes she used to keep in her own body heat.

By the time she was a teenager, Anita vowed that she would live a different life from that of her mother or grandmother. She was tired of the mixture of fear, anger, and resignation that goes along with dependence on welfare, and she certainly didn't want her own children to experience these negative emotions. Watching her mother wait eagerly by the mailbox every two weeks for their government check disgusted Anita. She was going to make it on her own and take control of her life.

Her mother applauded this resolve and encouraged her to better herself through education. Anita was sure that her mother's advice was right, and she diligently pursued her schoolwork despite the indifference of many of her peers. By the time she was in eighth grade, Anita was a straight-A student, and her teachers voted her the top pupil among her middle school classmates.

Her life took an unexpected turn when she met James, the older brother of her best friend from school. He was five years her senior, nearly twenty at the time, and Anita was flattered that such a handsome older boy found her attractive. They began dating soon after their first meeting, and they were inseparable after a few months. As their love matured, so did their physical relationship, and Anita discovered that she was pregnant a few weeks before her sixteenth birthday.

Anita's mother and grandmother were visibly shaken by this news. She was the one child for whom they had high hopes. Anita was expected to graduate from high school and go on to community college or vocational school to become a health-care professional. Now what was she going to do? Would she become one more generation of their family to subsist on welfare, living in the same impoverished community and exposing her own children to the same plight?

Anita viewed her situation quite differently. She and James were in love, and he vowed to stay by her side throughout the pregnancy and beyond. In contrast, she hardly knew her own father and had seen her grandfather only three times. James had steady work as a mechanic at a naval shipyard, while her father and grandfather were employed only sporadically. Although they couldn't afford to be together right away, their plan was to get married and find an apartment as soon as possible.

The next several months were spent preparing for the baby's arrival. Like most pregnant girls her age Anita quit school, but she promised her teachers and family that she would graduate or prepare for and take the high school equivalency exam when things settled down. James did remain at her side, but their plans to marry and live together were put on hold until the strike at the shipyard was resolved. Without a steady income, Anita would have to live with her relatives a bit longer.

By the time she gave birth to her son, the union had worked through its differences with management at the shipyard. Anita and James were married a few weeks later, and they moved into a two-bedroom apartment within walking distance of her family's residence. They considered other neighborhoods in their search for a home but decided to stay in the same community so that they would continue to receive support from their kin.

Over the course of the next several years, Anita had two additional children, both boys. Money was always tight, but she learned how to shop wisely and put every dollar of their limited income to its best use. On a few occasions Anita borrowed five or ten dollars from her mother or grandmother, but she always was able to pay them back with their next paycheck. Anita was proud of the life she and her husband had created. Their living arrangements were superior to the ones she had endured as a child, and they were making it on their own, without government support.

Unfortunately, the shipyard closed almost immediately after the birth of their third child. Congress and the military had argued about the necessity of a shipyard in this location for years, but they had always decided to leave it operational. The news that it had been selected for closure because of budget cutbacks sent shock waves through the community as several thousand people prepared to be laid off. In order to reduce this negative impact, local politicians invited employers from around the country to interview former employees of the yard. The only one interested in hiring James, however, was a representative of a factory located three hundred miles from their home.

Anita and James discussed their options, and they decided that it would be best for the family if James took the job. It would be a difficult transition—the children were at an age where the presence of their father was particularly important, so his absence would be hard for them to understand. Nonetheless, without a steady income at about the same level as that of the shipyard job, they would not be able to survive on their own. As James prepared to depart, he assured Anita that they would be reunited soon. They had a tearful goodbye one Sunday as James hopped on a bus and headed south to his new job.

Over the succeeding weeks, James was dutiful about sending most of his paycheck to Anita to support the family. Money was tighter than usual since they now lived apart and had to support two residences, so Anita began economizing further by shopping at local thrift and secondhand stores. She was more determined than ever to keep their family solvent until she and James could be together again.

However, things took a turn for the worse about six months later. James was transferred to a different work team, and he and his new supervisor mixed like oil and water. The supervisor was constantly critical of James, docking his pay when he returned from lunch two minutes late or held up production for a few seconds by wiping his brow. The conflict between them erupted one afternoon in a physical altercation, and James was fired as a result. He sent all of his final paycheck to Anita with a note of apology.

After that point, James began sending smaller amounts of money on a sporadic basis. Anita was truly frightened for the first time in their marriage. She had nothing in reserve and was unable even to pay the rent with the money he forwarded, much less the food and clothing bills. Additionally, with the loss of his job the family was now without health insurance, and Anita could not afford to purchase the medicine their asthmatic eldest son needed. James stopped answering the phone as her calls became increasingly frantic, and he eventually moved out of the room where he had been living without leaving a forwarding address. Anita had no one left to turn to but her mother and grandmother.

These two elders agreed that it was time for Anita and her family to go on welfare. They described the system of benefits that was available, including financial support, food stamps, and health insurance. Anita also might qualify for the Women, Infants, and Children (WIC) program, which provides supplemental food for mothers with young children. Since her family was about to be evicted from their apartment if they didn't make a payment soon, Anita had no other choice.

Her mother agreed to accompany her to the state welfare offices and help her navigate the bureaucratic maze of lines, forms, and interviews. She coached Anita to be patient and respectful. An incomplete form, improper remark, or aggressive response might result in ineligibility or a delay in the provision of assistance. The well-being of Anita's family was dependent upon her cooperation, and she was now at the mercy of the welfare system.

After several hours of answering preliminary questions, verifying her identity and that of her children, and explaining her financial situation, Anita was granted an interview with a benefits specialist. With no more than a perfunctory greeting, the specialist began asking her a series of intimate and probing questions: Where is your husband currently living? When was the last time you were in contact with him? Are you pregnant? Do you plan on having any additional children? Anita was flushed with anger at this inquisition, but she swallowed her pride for the sake of her children and provided short but accurate responses.

The conversation eventually turned to Anita's ability to support her family. What was the highest grade she had completed in school? What marketable skills did she have? As Anita formulated her responses to these questions, it dawned on her that she was incapable of providing for her family in this time of crisis. Who would hire a high school dropout lacking vocational training at a salary that would meet the material needs of her family? The answer was no one.

Anita finally realized that she was in the same trap as her mother and grandmother, and this identification with them horrified her. The children whom she and her husband cherished were now dependent upon the state for their survival, a system that Anita knew firsthand was insufficient. They were failures as parents, incapable of providing adequately for their own progeny. Also, Anita was now a single mother, one of hundreds of undifferentiated women in her community without regular support from the father of her offspring.

Living on Welfare

When all was said and done, Anita and her family were placed on the welfare rolls. At first she was relieved that their financial crisis was resolved. They would have a steady income, the ability to purchase food, and access to health care. However, on closer inspection Anita realized that there was no way they could survive on the budget established by the benefits specialist. It was unrealistic and too restrictive.

Anita had been good at math in school, and she used her knowledge of arithmetic to examine these numbers for herself.

The biweekly checks from the Aid to Families with Dependent Children (AFDC) program were only forty dollars above her monthly rent and utility payments, providing little additional income for clothing, phone service, public transportation, laundry, and toys for her children. Food stamps supplied about seventy-five cents per meal, and even Anita, who was frugal by nature and could stretch a dollar, was unable to figure out how to make them last for the whole month. Besides, food stamps couldn't be used for a host of additional goods for which she had no resources, including basic toiletries such as soap, toothpaste, and feminine hygiene products, and medicines not covered by the state health care plan like cough syrup and aspirin.

After a few months of living on welfare, her prediction of a severe shortfall became a reality. She worked out an arrangement with her landlord regarding back payments, and their home was secure for a while. However, even with the help of the WIC program there was never enough milk, meat, and produce in the house to satisfy her growing family. Anita ran out of diapers regularly, and the co-pay on her son's prescription medicine took almost one-fourth of her biweekly cash. They were now three months behind on their phone bill, and they were scheduled to have their service terminated in two weeks unless they paid the full amount.

To make matters worse, her children were reaching the age when they begin expressing desires for the myriad products available within our society. Almost daily Anita would hear from one of the older boys that he wanted a particular toy he had seen on television, to go to the latest Disney movie, or to have dinner at McDonald's and get a Happy Meal. She briefly considered getting rid of their television set altogether in order to limit their urges, but she decided against it when she realized that it was their primary form of entertainment.

Anita even stopped taking her children to the local mall, one of the few outings the family enjoyed, particularly in cold weather. Initially the four of them would wander in and out of a variety of stores, absorbing the sights and sounds and other forms of stimulation. However, in recent months her kids had begun touching everything and pleading with her to buy them something in just about every store. Anita tried to reduce their requests by window shopping rather than going in the stores themselves, but the vendors in the hallways of the mall seemed to have just as many tempting products. It would cost Anita $7.50 to purchase one helium-filled balloon for each of her children, an amount she could not afford to spend on such a frivolous item. The only alternative was to quit going to the mall unless absolutely necessary.

Holidays and birthdays during their first year on welfare were particularly traumatic for the children. For example, her eldest son turned six while attending kindergarten that year, and he begged his mother to let him have a party like the ones some of the other kids in his class had. His fantasy included guests, presents, party favors, cake and ice cream, and a trip to the local arcade. Anita estimated that the minimum cost for such an event would be sixty-five dollars, more than her available cash for a variety of necessities for the entire month. No matter how she did the math, it just wasn't possible to afford a party without great hardship, so she told him he would have to wait until his seventh birthday.

Christmas was even worse. For months in advance, the television paraded an endless series of programs and commercials before her children's eyes which showed Santa Claus and loving families enjoying the holiday season. These scenes typically contained beautifully adorned trees, brightly colored seasonal decorations, and individually selected gifts that demonstrated either the family members' love for one another or the fact that the children had been good all year long. Anita's children anxiously asked for her reassurance that they had behaved properly during the year so that Santa would come to their house with his bag full of toys. They also were concerned that the small tree and meager decorations in their home didn't display the proper Christmas spirit. Anita told them that they were all good boys and that Santa Claus came without regard for the quality of the decor in a home.

These interactions broke Anita's heart, and she did everything in her power to make the holidays as special as possible. She registered her children through the local Catholic church to receive gifts from a more affluent community in a nearby suburb. The presents were delivered a few days before Christmas, and they were beautifully wrapped. Unfortunately, they were items like socks, underwear, and gloves—real necessities that Anita had specifically asked for because of her children's limited wardrobes but not items that they would find very exciting under a Christmas tree.

Anita also went to the local Salvation Army to attend their annual holiday toy giveaway. At this event she was able to examine hundreds of used and donated items in search of gifts for each of her children. She was allowed only one toy per child, so she spent hours looking through the bins in order to find presents for her boys that were as close as possible to the things they desired.

Inevitably the day was a disappointment for everybody. All three children rose early, with her eldest son leading the charge. As they looked at the meager number of gifts under the tree, Anita could sense the drop in their enthusiasm level. Each child had two presents to open, but neither gift was very exciting or desirable. The holiday meal was similarly uninspiring, with few additions beyond their ordinary evening meals. As Anita had expected, her eldest son asked what happened and why Santa Claus had ignored the Christmas list he had so carefully prepared and mailed to the North Pole. She responded that Santa wasn't able to make it to their apartment this year, but he promised to bring them extra gifts next time around. This reply satisfied the boy's curiosity for the moment, but Anita wondered what she would tell him if things failed to improve by the following holiday season.

Anita began to feel overwhelmed by feelings of deprivation. In virtually every important aspect of her life, she was unable to do or have the things that she and her family truly needed. The problems with special occasions were just the tip of the iceberg. Now that her eldest child was in kindergarten, how would she be able to outfit him with the clothing and school supplies that would allow him to fit in with his classmates and do what his teachers asked of him? How would she afford these items when all three of her children were in school? Anita also was constantly making a tradeoff between buying limited amounts of healthy foods that cost more, such as milk, and purchasing a more abundant supply of cheaper and less healthy substitutes, such as Kool-Aid. By the end of the month, she literally had no choice—it was the cheaper goods or nothing at all. As her children continued to grow, Anita worried that the situation would get increasingly dire.

She tried to reason with her caseworker during their periodic meetings on the status of her support. Anita would present to this woman an accounting of the money and benefits she received against her fixed bills and other necessities. Since it was clear to both of them that her income was insufficient, why couldn't her support level be raised? Anita tired of hearing over and over again how the benefit amounts were precisely set and that the caseworker had little or no discretion. Who would establish such a standard given the cost of food, clothing, and shelter in their community? Why was the system designed without the flexibility to help people meet their most basic needs? Anita was left feeling angry and frustrated.

These meetings also caused her to feel insecure and as if she were losing control of her family's destiny. Each appointment opened with the same series of questions. Have you heard from your husband? Has he or anyone else provided you with support of any kind? Are you now living with someone (such as a boyfriend) who is helping you pay your bills? Are you pregnant? Do you realize that you will *not* receive further benefits to support additional children? Anita clearly understood that a wrong answer or an inappropriate remark might cause her current level of support to drop or be removed all together. She felt as if she were in front of her mother as a young child, only this time the "parent" was an uncaring bureaucrat. Anita felt naked, completely exposed to this woman, with her family's survival in this stranger's hands. Even her own sexuality was no longer her private affair.

As if getting and keeping her benefits weren't enough trouble, using them also was difficult. When Anita went shopping for groceries, typically with her children in tow, she painstakingly selected products to maximize the use of her food stamps. However, she invariably would have some ineligible items among her selections, and the clerk would let her know, using a sarcastic or arrogant tone. One time when she was at a supermarket outside her own neighborhood, the checkout clerk shouted across the store to the manager that she needed food stamp change. Anita was sure that everyone in the building heard this woman's request, branding her and her children as poor. On these occasions, Anita was left feeling ashamed and humiliated.

The provision of health care through the welfare system was no better. For example, when Anita told an attending physician at the local hospital that Medicaid covered her son's expenses, his manner changed and his recommended course of treatment was drastically reduced. The doctor suddenly was in a hurry to dismiss the child from his charge, and he was uninterested in doing any additional testing. It was clear to Anita that her son was no better off than he had been before their trip to the hospital. Anita was unsure why this attitudinal shift had occurred, but she assumed that the medical coverage for welfare recipients in her state entitled a family to less than adequate treatment and a concomitant lack of respect. They were stigmatized as inferior or unworthy.

Taken together, these feelings of deprivation, anger, frustration, loss of control, shame, humiliation, and inferiority caused Anita to become increasingly alienated from mainstream society. What did she and her family have in common with the typical middle-class family that was portrayed by the media? Anita and her children had little access to the things such families took for granted, and they were unlikely to have them in the future. Sometimes Anita would see families in places like the mall wearing their nice clothes and going shopping. They were working people who earned a living by doing something important. They often looked tired, but they had self-esteem because they were dependent only on themselves.

To make matters worse, her children were beginning to suffer as a result of this deprivation. The nurse who came monthly to the school reported to Anita that her children were underweight and looked anemic. She recommended several changes to their diet as well as an expensive multivitamin, but Anita knew that both were impossible given the financial restrictions she faced. Her children also began acting up on trips to the supermarket because of their own frustrations at seeing all that was available yet inaccessible to them. Anita sensed they recognized that kids within their own neighborhood had different levels of affluence, with the children of welfare mothers typically at the bottom of the scale.

Anita feared that this situation would eventually extinguish the bright light of their childhood, with corresponding negative physical and emotional outcomes. For the first time in her life she experienced the sense of hopelessness and despair that is a classic symptom of clinical depression. She was tired all the time, and even getting out of bed in the morning and attending to her children's most basic needs was difficult. This first year on the welfare rolls was the most grueling in her life, and she felt as if she were falling down a deep hole that had no discernable bottom. Anita could imagine no way out of her current problems, and she was becoming increasingly resigned to her status as a welfare mother.

Coping with Welfare Living

Things began to improve when her mother and grandmother intervened. These women starting coming to Anita's home to relieve her of some of her daily chores. They washed and dressed the children, cleaned the kitchen, and purchased food, diapers, and clothing on a regular basis. They also took over the expense of her son's medicine, ensuring that he would be well enough to attend most of his classes now that he was in the first grade. This initial support helped Anita realize that she wasn't alone in the world, and her mood brightened for the first time in months.

More importantly, they listened to and commiserated with Anita. The three women talked about the impossibility of making it on one's own while on welfare. They agreed that the restrictions on one's material life were severe, and that the resulting stress was damaging to one's health. They shared many horror stories about and problems with life on welfare, and Anita felt a sense of kinship with them that she never had previously.

This initial boost caused Anita to reach out and seek other forms of emotional support within her community. She returned to her church for the first time in years, and she prayed regularly that her situation, and that of her children, would continue to improve. Each Sunday she would bring her kids to the children's mass, and they would interact and sing with other families who lived under similar conditions. She developed a sense of camaraderie with these families which helped reduce her feelings of alienation from the outside world.

Her pastor invited her to join the parish support group for single mothers, and Anita eagerly accepted. This group met in the church basement every other Wednesday, and their meetings provided a forum for these women to discuss the quality of their lives. At times these discussions degenerated into nothing more than "bitching" sessions, where the women complained about their caseworkers, benefits levels, children, and the men who roamed in and out of their lives. However, when this occurred their priest would attempt to improve the quality of their conversation by reciting the title of a book called *There's a Lot of Month Left at the End of the Money* and asking how they coped with this problem.

The women typically would laugh at his remarks and then launch into lengthy presentations of their own survival strategies. Some of the mothers discussed a form of self-deception by which they took a small amount of their cash benefits or food stamps and placed them in an out-of-the-way place until they were desperate. They only borrowed from this stash in an emergency or when all other sources were exhausted. If they made it until a day or two before their checks arrived, they used the money or stamps to buy their families a special treat.

The women also discussed their side jobs and under-the-table employment schemes that helped them stay solvent. Child care or babysitting in one's home was a common occupation that the women could hold without neglecting their own children. Others cleaned homes in more affluent communities, especially on weekends when they could have a friend or relative watch their kids. Still others worked in the evenings at local bars and restaurants after their children went to sleep. In order to avoid paying taxes or losing benefits, they often earned only tips or were paid a modest wage in cash at the end of the night. A much smaller group admitted to selling drugs or prostitution as a way to make ends meet, and although they expressed some remorse, they felt justified since their goal was to help their families.

During and after these meetings Anita would take a few moments to reflect on their meaning to her life and her family. A whole new set of income-generating opportunities was available that might allow her to supplement their welfare benefits so that their buying power would be at a tolerable level. It was technically illegal for such money to go unreported to one's caseworker, but Anita recognized that this dishonesty had to be balanced against a family's material well-being. If she reported the money, her benefits would be reduced by the same amount, leaving them with a net gain of zero. Additionally, she began to realize that the image of the disreputable welfare mother who indulges herself while ignoring the needs of her children was not representative of her or many other women in her community. They cared deeply for their children, and most of their waking hours were spent trying to improve their kids' lives. Some welfare mothers abused the system, but Anita was not one of them, and this recognition bolstered her sense of self.

The support from her elders also allowed Anita to enjoy some private time away from her children and their current situation. She began taking long walks through her neighborhood and a local park, sometimes traveling for hours enjoying the freedom of movement. During these trips she allowed her mind to wander, and she began to dream about a better world. She envisioned her family living in a modest three-bedroom house in one of the better suburban areas outside the city. The kitchen was nicely equipped with a stove, oven, and microwave, and the boys' bedrooms contained all the toys they needed. Anita had her own bathroom where she could take hot baths after a long day. A swing set and trampoline were in the back yard, and a fence to keep in their pet dog surrounded it.

On one of these walks Anita crossed paths with a handsome young man whom she had known in her previous life as a student. They recognized each other immediately and spent almost an hour catching up on what had happened in their lives over the years. Anita discussed her children with pride and described their futures using a positive tone. He said that he was divorced but without children, and that he was working full-time at the local post office.

Over the next several weeks they spent an increasing amount of time in each other's company, often doing things together with her children. He seemed to enjoy being with her kids and playing the role of father, and he even began giving her a few dollars each payday to help them buy food. Eventually, he also started paying her phone bill so that she would be able to use her limited cash elsewhere. Anita felt a bit guilty not reporting this additional income to her caseworker, but she rationalized her deceit as being in her family's best interest. As their relationship progressed, they decided to maintain separate residences so that her welfare benefits wouldn't be jeopardized.

Even with the support of her new man, things remained tight. Her second child was getting ready to go to school, and Anita could hardly believe the amount of food that the three of them ate. Anita knew that other welfare families faced a similar situation, so she organized the women from her support group into a cooperative that helped each member financially with a few dollars or with some stamps when necessary. Additionally, Anita started working for one of these women on Saturdays cleaning houses. She worked only in the morning, from 8:00 A.M. until noon so that the babysitting burden on her mother and grandmother wasn't too great. Her total revenue from this half-day's work was just fifteen dollars, but it put her over the top with regard to her regular bills.

Anita also learned how to acquire a variety of products through the private social welfare system at little or no cost. She found places where she could receive donated clothing for free, and these items supplemented the clothes that she purchased for her children and herself from discount retailers and thrift stores. The Salvation Army and some local church groups sold a variety of used household items such as fans, microwave ovens, and beds at very low prices. Anita was able to find affordable beds at these places for her two youngest sons when they moved out of their cribs. Finally, food was more widely available than Anita ever realized. In addition to the deliveries to her church from its sister parish in a more affluent suburb, the community action agency in her neighborhood collected excess foodstuffs from supermarkets, bakeries, and restaurants and distributed it from the local office. All Anita had to do was show up on Thursday mornings and she could fill two shopping bags with food for her family.

Anita began to feel that she was turning the corner on her life. She had a new and better relationship with her extended family, and the financial as well as emotional support they provided was greatly appreciated. Her friends from church and her man also gave assistance, and they encouraged her to take back control of her life. While welfare still played a dominant role in her day-to-day existence, Anita had discovered ways to extend its support to an almost livable level. The psychological burden she had carried since her husband's disappearance was lifting, and she could feel a sense of relief wash over her.

Changes due to Welfare Reform

Anita recognized that things were changing when the top stories in the local media were about welfare reform. She heard the slogan "ending welfare as we know it," but was unsure what it meant. Clearly welfare was a failure in that it did not provide a reasonable material life for the needy women and children in her community. However, she was certain that her understanding of welfare was not the same as that of the middle-class politicians who were engaged in this debate. How many of them bought their food using stamps? Did their families ever try to receive adequate medical care through Medicaid?

At her next meeting with her caseworker, Anita asked if her benefit levels might change as a result of the reform movement. The caseworker answered by painting a disturbing picture. She noted that the average citizen believes that most American adults should support themselves as well as their children through work. The politicians had picked up on this theme, and they were determined to limit welfare benefits to the truly needy over a predetermined period of time.

Anita agreed with the idea of limiting welfare, but she felt that her situation suggested that she *was* truly needy. She had young children, an absent spouse, and poor job prospects. She wasn't wasting the money on drugs or frivolous items, and she was supplementing her benefits through her own efforts. From her perspective, welfare was designed to help people just like her. Further, how did time limits make sense? Each family's situation was different, requiring a benefit level and time period responsive to the individual situation. Such a constraint seemed like one more unnecessary restriction that might reduce the quality of life and self-esteem of welfare families.

A few months after this discussion, the state welfare office informed Anita that she would have to enroll in one of their work readiness programs or find employment within the next review cycle. Failure to do so could result in the termination of her benefits. While she tried to prepare herself in advance for such changes, Anita was unsure how to proceed now that the direction was clear. Her grandmother might be able to watch her children, although Anita was uncertain whether she had the time to supervise her remaining preschooler. However, she knew that there was no money available for transportation to and from a program or job, and her limited wardrobe would be inappropriate for either situation.

Her caseworker was required to meet with her and discuss these options, and Anita scheduled an appointment with some trepidation. During their meeting the caseworker suggested that Anita enter the training program for the high school equivalency examination (General Education Development, or GED). She noted that the other vocational and placement programs required a high school diploma as an entrance requirement. Anita felt a mixture of anxiety and excitement about returning to school after so many years, but her real concerns were with child care and incidental costs. However, her caseworker assured her that supplemental funds for these expenses were available, and that Anita was eligible for them as long as she remained a student in good standing.

Two months later Anita was enrolled in classes with a private firm that did GED preparation. With the money provided to support her efforts, she could afford to place her youngest son in a private day-care center near her home, buy some new work clothes, and take the bus to and from the training center. Anita was nervous on her first day, but her enthusiasm for the program improved when her scores on the math and reading achievement tests revealed that she was functioning at the twelfth-grade level. It may have been a long time, but the good student in her background was still there.

The next twelve weeks were hectic for Anita and her family. They settled into a grueling routine, which began promptly at 6:00 A.M. and continued without a break until after the evening meal. The early morning hours were spent in preparation for school, and Anita moved from child to child combing hair, brushing teeth, and tying shoes. As the children settled down to their breakfast, she jumped in the shower, toweled off, and quickly applied her makeup. While dressing, Anita shouted orders at the boys to make sure that they had all of their school supplies properly stored in their backpacks.

Anita ushered her brood out the door at precisely 7:45 A.M., and she deposited her oldest sons at school and her youngest at day care by 8:00 A.M. The bus picked her up at approximately 8:10 A.M., and she was seated at her desk in the training center within twenty minutes. Classes continued uninterrupted until 11:30 A.M., at which time Anita spent thirty minutes taking practice tests on various sections of the GED exam. She then walked down the street to the local coffee shop, purchased a cup of coffee and a bagel, and boarded the bus for a return trip to her neighborhood.

After arriving home, she went immediately to retrieve her youngest son from day care as well as her middle son from kindergarten. Depending upon the weather, they spent the next few hours either playing in a nearby park or watching television at home. At this point, the three of them returned to school to pick up her eldest son from his full-day program. They re-entered their apartment, and Anita and her oldest child spent the next hour working together on his homework. She felt it was essential that her children understand the importance of doing well and staying in school, and she wanted to make this point with her words and actions.

After the evening meal, the children watched their favorite television programs while Anita prepared her lessons for the next day's classes. Her kids went to bed by 9:00 P.M., and Anita spent the next hour washing dishes, picking up and cleaning clothes, and preparing for another day filled with the same challenges. She continued her housecleaning job on Saturdays—there was little choice given her current financial situation. However, Sundays were a day of rest, and Anita spent time with her family and her new man, typically eating dinner out at a local fast-food restaurant.

At the end of her term, she took and successfully passed all sections of the GED exam. Anita was thrilled with this accomplishment, and she was relieved finally to have fulfilled her pledge to her family and teachers to complete her high school education. She began to fantasize about a career as a working professional for the first time in her adult life. Anita could imagine herself in the white uniform of a health-care worker, moving from person to person and providing medical and emotional support. Her children would look up to her and brag to their friends about how their mother helped sick people become well. They might even be able to afford a house like the one she had dreamed about previously. Anita would no longer dread birthdays and holidays. Instead, they would be special events filled with the material goods that her children desired and deserved.

She discussed the next step with her caseworker, and they discovered that many of the vocational programs offered by the state were unavailable due to funding problems. As a result, Anita entered training to become an office assistant rather than a health-care worker. She was disappointed initially at this change in career paths, but she bolstered herself by noting that she could always look for a job in a physician's office.

This training program required the same hurried routine as her GED preparation, and Anita began to feel her enthusiasm and energy levels fall. The daily classes were less stimulating than before, focusing on dress, deportment, and the use of basic voice and data communications technology. Unfortunately, neither the phone system nor the computers in her classroom were state of the art, and her teachers were unable to show her how to use the latest programming features or software. As a result, Anita was instructed to become familiar with the computer keyboard layout and practice her typing skills as often as possible.

Upon completion of her training, Anita was placed with a local retailer who received a subsidy for six months as part of the state's welfare-to-work program. Anita was employed as the office receptionist, answering the phone and doing simple clerical tasks from 8:30 A.M. until 12:30 P.M. during the workweek. She would be on probation for this period, but the job had the potential to become full-time depending upon her performance and the continuation of funding. These duties seemed uninteresting to Anita, but she felt she had no choice but to accept the offer. She would start work on the following Monday.

The job paid six dollars an hour, with two dollars of this wage subsidized by the government. Anita's cash benefits were reduced by four dollars for every hour worked, so her net gain after taxes was minimal. Her employer provided no health-care coverage, but the state agreed to allow her family to remain on Medicaid for the next six months. The child care, transportation, and clothing allowances allocated during her training also were in effect; however, they would be phased out over the next nine months. The goal was to have Anita and her family independent of the public welfare system within one year of the start of her new career.

Anita entered this stage of her life with mixed emotions. It would feel good to be working and earning money through legitimate employment for the first time, and she could see that her extended family took pride in her efforts to move off the welfare rolls. However, she was in a low-paying job that was subsidized by the state, and its continuation after the funding stopped was uncertain. Even if it became a full-time opportunity, the money Anita would earn after taxes was not significantly more than she received while on welfare. As important, the health benefits, child care and clothing allowances, and transportation funding were essential to making this whole thing work. Once they disappeared, Anita felt certain that she would not be able to survive.

Her first few weeks on the job were particularly challenging. Taking orders from so many different people was difficult for Anita, who had never worked in a similar environment previously. The men and women who worked around her were from backgrounds and communities different from her own, and Anita felt like an outsider when they stopped and chatted with each other. While she couldn't prove it, she was certain they were aware of her status as a welfare mother, and they remained physically and emotionally distant as a result. On occasion one of her children would be sick and Anita would stay home to help him. When she phoned to tell her bosses that she would not be in that day, Anita invariably received a call from her caseworker, who was checking up to make sure her excuse was legitimate.

As she reflected on her life, Anita felt pride that she was raising three good boys, had cared for them during much of their lives without the support of her spouse, and had completed her schooling as well as a vocational training program. Nonetheless, the restrictions she saw in her future were as severe as the constraints she experienced while on welfare. Her job provided no more income than her former cash benefits, yet she now was unable to spend as much quality time with her children, especially the youngest. No better opportunities or job prospects were on the horizon, yet the loss of other forms of support such as child care was imminent. Anita recognized and appreciated her personal courage to move forward, but she was uncertain whether she could truly go it alone. In the back of her mind she kept asking the same nagging question: Was her family better off on welfare?

SUGGESTED READINGS

This chapter was informed by:

Hill, Ronald Paul, and Debra Lynn Stephens (1997), "Impoverished Consumers and Consumer Behavior: The Case of AFDC Mothers," *Journal of Macromarketing* 17 (Fall), 32–48.

Hill, Ronald Paul, and Sandi Macan (1996), "Consumer Survival on Welfare with an Emphasis on Medicaid and the Food Stamp Program," *Journal of Public Policy and Marketing* 15 (Spring), 118–27.

Of further interest:

Epstein, William M. (1997), *Welfare in America: How Social Science Fails the Poor*, Madison: University of Wisconsin Press. The author traces the social welfare proposals of the late twentieth century, and he examines their validity in the face of social scientific evidence. He finds that liberal and conservative approaches vary only in their generosity, and that both are based on the principle that "economic self-sufficiency is socially desirable." Yet while our society has long believed that requiring work is the best way to reduce poverty, such a simple solution is not supported by the preponderance of research. In fact, the author shows that such a middle-class ideal fails in the face of a lack of middle-class opportunities for the poor. Unfortunately, allocating the resources necessary to improve their circumstances to a level consistent with more affluent citizens is politically infeasible. Thus, the author suggests that we are moving toward greater inequity in schools, jobs, and other essential living conditions, further eroding the prospects for the impoverished within our nation.

Gilens, Martin (1999), *Why Americans Hate Welfare: Race, Media, and the Politics of Antipoverty Policy*, Chicago: University of Chicago Press. The author of this book examines why one of the richest nations in the world allows millions of its citizens to go without basic consumer commodities on a regular basis. The underlying cause is the highly prejudiced and racially skewed views of middle-class Americans concerning the poor. According to this perspective, the media is the real culprit because of its negative portrayal of welfare recipients as blacks who prefer to live off government handouts rather than work. This stereotype results in misinformation about the true ethnic composition and motivations of people in poverty, and it leads the general public to regard most welfare families as undeserving. Nonetheless, Americans do want their government to provide more for the poor, but a clear political mandate will not exist until the public's perception of the impoverished mirrors the poor's lived experience.

Handler, Joel F., and Lucie White (1999), *Hard Labor: Women and Work in the Post-Welfare Era*, Armonk, N.Y.: M. E. Sharpe. This book provides case studies by scholars and political activists which are grounded in the lives of low-income working women. These cases concentrate on barriers that keep poor women from thriving in waged work, policy innovations that eliminate these barriers, and strategies for implementing these policies which partner with impoverished women. Chapters are written by different authors, and topics include barriers to finding and keeping jobs, self-employment opportunities and pitfalls, the need for quality child care, health insurance coverage for the working poor, and community-based employment services. The volume closes with a provocative chapter that looks at the prospects for low-waged women within the context of the globally competitive labor market.

Zucchino, Davis (1997), *Myth of the Welfare Queen: A Pulitzer Prize-Winning Journalist's Portrait of Women on the Line*, New York: Scribner. In this volume the author examines the consumer existence of welfare mothers and families prior to the introduction of

AFDC/welfare reform. For six months he followed the lives of several single mothers trying to determine how they fed and clothed their children and obtained medical care, and whether they looked for jobs. He found no evidence of the publicly despised "Cadillac-driving, champagne-sipping, penthouse-living welfare queens." Instead, he discovered a thriving community of impoverished women who fend for themselves, spending their lives seeking food, clothing, and secure housing. These resourceful women lived from one welfare check to the next, and they supplemented their income by picking through trash, doing odd jobs, and shopping at thrift shops.

SIX

Rural Poor
Tammy and Her Momma

We'd get up before sun-up to get the work done up
We'd work in the fields till the sun had gone down
We've stood and we've cried as we helplessly watched
A hailstorm a'beaten our crops to the ground
We've gone to bed hungry many nights in the past
In the good old days when times were bad

I've seen daddy's hands break open and bleed
And I've seen him work till he's stiff as a board
An' I've seen momma layin' in suffer and sickness
In need of a Doctor we couldn't afford
Anything at all was more than we had
In the good old days when times were bad
          —Dolly Parton, "In the Good Old Days
           (When Times Were Bad)"

The rural poor in our country have received considerably less attention from the media as well as the academic community than the urban poor have. Nonetheless, approximately 9 million Americans living in rural communities were impoverished at any one time during the 1990s, representing about 25 percent of all poor citizens. This group is geographically diverse, with significant pockets of rural poverty existing in every region of the nation.

111

This chapter focuses on poverty in an Appalachian coal-mining community whose members struggle to meet their daily consumer needs. Their lives are affected greatly by the lack of decent jobs, poor housing conditions, air and water pollution, limited alternatives for goods and services, and physical isolation. Taken together, these factors suggest that the rural poor face an imbalance in their exchange relationships with product providers, making them vulnerable to manipulation, deception, and poor treatment.

The results of this investigation suggest a more differentiated portrait of their lives. Through an examination of three types of resources—economic, cultural, and social—this study demonstrates that the rural poor are not disempowered victims. Instead, they have a variety of resource deficits as well as strengths that define and affect their relationship with the marketplace. For example, rural citizens often have limited economic capital and are more likely to live in poverty and be under- or unemployed than typical citizens. Additionally, their communities may lack cultural capital, with lower levels of literacy, high school graduation rates, and transferable skills than the national averages. However, their social capital may be strong. Appalachia has a long history of struggle against powerful outside forces, and individuals often have sought solace and support through churches, extended family, and friends. As a result, the people of Appalachia stress the importance of community, reciprocity in dealing with others, and egalitarianism in social interactions.

The chapter concentrates much attention on one aspect of the rural poor's consumer lives: interactions with the health-care system. Because of the region's isolation, the availability of providers is limited. Additionally, as a result of poverty, access to appropriate services and medications is constrained. Finally, because of the cultural differences between the rural poor and highly educated health-care practitioners, interactions often are unsatisfying and unproductive. A prominent exception to the pattern revealed in this study is that of the health mobile, which provided a unique blend of medical and emotional support within the focal community consistent with Appalachian values and norms.

TAMMY AND HER MOMMA

The Early Years

Tammy grew up in a small rural community located in a valley adjacent to an extensive mountain range. Her earliest memories of the town were of a bustling area, with a new school, store, or building always under construction. Families from all over the hills moved there in search of jobs in the coal mines as well as in the supporting industries, and a neighborhood of especially large and glamorous homes was built to house the owners and managers who ran these firms. Tammy's family was neither rich nor poor, but they had most of the things they needed to live a reasonable life.

They resided on a small farm about a mile from the center of town. This property had once been part of a larger working farm that had been owned by her grandfather and his family for generations. Upon his death, this land was divided into several sections, one for each of his surviving children, and Tammy's father was bequeathed a five-acre parcel. Although it was too small for real farming, they were able to plant a large vegetable and fruit garden, raise some livestock such as cows and chickens, and have a private retreat from the outside world.

Over time three brothers and three sisters joined the family as it expanded in size to a total of nine people. As the oldest sibling, Tammy took responsibility for many of the household chores, and there were times when her brothers and sisters seemed as if they were her own brood. She cleaned the kitchen after their morning and evening meals, sweeping the floors and washing and drying the dishes. Tammy was also responsible for making her siblings' school lunches, getting them off to the correct bus on time, and ensuring that they were properly groomed. In the afternoons Tammy would often join her mother on the farm, tending to the animals, weeding the garden, and harvesting ripe fruits and vegetables.

During these early hectic years, Tammy rarely had time to consider her individual needs and desires. After attending to her siblings, she seldom remembered to make her own lunch or properly prepare herself for school. On many occasions she worked with her brothers and sisters to make sure their homework was completed appropriately, but she failed to do her own. As a result Tammy was a marginal student who moved from grade to grade because of her sweet demeanor rather than her academic performance. She quit school at sixteen so that she could focus exclusively on her family responsibilities. Tammy never resented this decision. She was "duty bound" to help her momma.

While Tammy and her mother had primary responsibility for the home, her father earned a living by working in the coal mines. He was raised on the family farm as a boy, and he became a strong and decent man who wasn't afraid of hard work. When he returned from the war in Europe he continued working for his father, but this option ended when the larger farm was divided following his father's death two years later. Then he followed the legions of men who marched into the mines each day.

It was grueling, difficult, and dirty work, but the men were proud of their efforts and enjoyed making union wages. They recognized that their success and safety were dependent upon their operating as a cohesive unit, and a sense of trust and camaraderie developed among them. When an accident occurred, they rallied around their fellow worker and his family, providing financial, material, and emotional support. As a group they knew that the owners and managers of the mines took most of the profit but were subject to few of the physical risks. Nonetheless, despite these inequities and dangers the mines represented the best possible standard of living for men whose primary skill was a willingness to work hard.

Tammy's parents knew each other from their early school days, but they had little contact after the war. They became reacquainted at a dance in a local church basement which was sponsored by the miners' union, and they became inseparable after a few weeks of courting. They married almost exactly one year after that dance, and Tammy was born ten months later. Her mother experienced some difficulty getting pregnant a second time, and it was several years before a second child was born. After that birth, the other five children came at intervals of about twelve months.

The children's home life was rather uneventful during most of their childhood, and they experienced remarkable stability in their lives. However, after the children were grown, their father developed a serious respiratory problem that continued to worsen over time. He began experiencing difficulty breathing normally while on the job, and he quickly tired doing ordinary activities around the house. The union doctor examined him and explained that he had a chronic and debilitating lung disease that would decrease his functioning with age. He was forced to retire from the job and live on disability at age fifty-five.

With this change in their financial situation, Tammy's parents could no longer afford to pay the bills associated with their family home. An investor who was interested in developing the property made a bid for the five-acre parcel, and her father grudgingly agreed to sell the land to him. Tammy's parents took the money and purchased a two-bedroom mobile home in a park a few miles away. Her father's health continued to deteriorate over the next several years, and he refused to leave the house except for very special occasions, embarrassed by his physical weakness. By the time he died, he was unable to breathe without support.

A Family of Her Own

All three of Tammy's brothers followed their father into the mines after completing as much school as the law required of them. They enjoyed the sports in their small town, but they never took their schoolwork seriously. Every young man in their community knew his destiny was the mines. The only alternatives were services that supported the mines' activities, but few men wished to be on the sidelines.

One day they brought an older buddy from the mines by the family home to meet their oldest sister. Tammy had seen the man during her last year in school, and she remembered that he was a star receiver on the high school football team. After this initial meeting, they dated a few times before deciding just to be friends. However, after they had been apart for several months they began to miss each other, and they became engaged six months later.

They married and moved into a modest two-bedroom home built by the mining company to house its employees. It was within walking distance of the mines, giving Tammy an opportunity to keep up with her brothers and father as they traveled back and forth from work. Over the course of the next several years, Tammy and her husband had three children, two boys and a girl. Tammy raised all three children with the same care and attention that she had shown her siblings during their childhood.

Her children experienced their town much differently from the way Tammy had during her own early years. By the time they were in grade school, the mines were beginning a slow decline that would ultimately rob the community of its largest employer. This deterioration became evident everywhere, from the quality of the holiday celebrations downtown to the physical plant of the schools to retail stores in the surrounding area. Job loss among the men was a problem for the first time in Tammy's memory, and some former miners turned to the local bars with their unemployment checks to drown their frustrations with liquor. The once beautiful athletic fields where the community had turned out every Friday evening during the fall to cheer on the high school football team hadn't been properly cared for in years. Even the movie theater downtown closed because of a lack of business. The only remaining restaurants were fast-food places.

Tammy's sons were particularly troubled by this turn of events, and they vowed to leave town at the earliest opportunity. When her oldest son completed high school, he packed his few belongings and some clothing and headed for a large Southern city that was experiencing tremendous growth. He took a job in the construction business and learned a trade, working on the skyscrapers that were popping up in the commercial district. When the second son completed his schooling, he followed his brother to the same city to ply the same trade.

Tammy was constantly worried about her boys. She imagined that all kinds of horrors existed in such a place, including crime, drugs, and prostitution. Would her boys succumb to the temptations that existed in such a large city? Who would make sure they were safe, well fed, and healthy? She prayed for them every day and looked forward to their one or two visits a year. They invited her to visit as well, but she was too frightened to do so. All those people and that noise and congestion made her nervous. Tammy realized that she would be uncomfortable outside of her familiar surroundings.

Her daughter, on the other hand, stayed close to home. She had been a good student through high school but lacked the confidence and worldliness to attend college. Instead, she took a job at the local Wal-Mart and moved into a small apartment with two of her closest girlfriends. Three years later she met a young shop teacher from the high school, and they got married right away. They had one daughter and lived in a cozy three-bedroom house on the outskirts of town. Tammy was very proud of her daughter and delighted that she had married a man with long-term employment prospects.

At about the same time her youngest child left home, the mines stopped all operations on a permanent basis. Tammy's husband was one of the last men laid off by management, and they were fortunate to have a steady income during those final days. Of course, they were forced to leave their family home because the mining company owned it. The management offered to sell it to Tammy and her husband, but they were unable to afford it without a source of income other than the meager severance pay negotiated by the union.

Tammy's husband began collecting unemployment benefits like the rest of the former miners, and he looked diligently throughout their small community for a new job. Nothing he was offered came close to paying a salary that was equivalent to his union wages in the mines. Nonetheless, he tried a variety of positions in local service and retail establishments over the next several years in order to survive and to avoid relying on welfare payments for his livelihood. With the additional money Tammy made working part-time in fast-food restaurants and in a nonunion sewing factory, they eked out a living.

They initially considered moving to a larger community where more opportunities existed, but they decided against such a drastic change. This town was their home and many of their friends from childhood still lived there. Relatives going back for generations in their families were buried in the local cemetery, and Tammy and her husband planned to be buried next to them when their time came. They had known financial difficulties before, especially during union strikes by the miners, and they had survived. Anyway, Tammy's momma was widowed and alone, and it was Tammy's responsibility to look after her. As a result, the two of them rented a home in the same trailer park as Tammy's mother so that they would be close by if she needed them.

Present-day Life

When Tammy reflected on what had happened to her community during her lifetime, she experienced mixed emotions. She sadly recalled when the mines abandoned their operations and the financial basis upon which the town was dependent nearly disappeared. More than half of all adult men in her community eventually worked for the mines in one capacity or another during their heyday. Additionally, most of the restaurants, grocery stores, recreation centers, and the school system were dependent upon this revenue base for their survival. When the mines closed, most of the jobs in these support services vanished as well.

The men her husband's age or older spent months or years looking for a job that might replace most or all of their lost wages. However, with the contraction of industry in general, the total pool of higher-wage positions had shrunk accordingly. Thus, this group of hard-working and proud men was reduced to living on unemployment benefits or to accepting entry-level positions in the few remaining service firms at drastically reduced incomes. A few moved to other parts of the country in search of the diminishing number of mining jobs, but the majority stayed put. They were too old to try something new but too young to retire. In the end, most accepted their lot in life, lowered their standard of living, and grew old before their time.

The younger men and women were a different story. Those who were already working in the mines and had families, mortgages, and more extensive connections in the community struggled like their older counterparts. However, their youth and vigor gave them a step up in the labor market, and they were more likely to get the available jobs. Those individuals without family ties and those just coming of working age often left permanently, causing a net migration out of an entire generational cohort. Tammy realized that her own sons were an example of the disaffection of youth within their community.

This financial collapse caused a drastic reduction in the funding of infrastructure projects, and the whole community seemed to sag. Roads, sidewalks, signage, and municipal buildings were years behind schedule in needed repairs, posing hazards for vehicles and people alike. The sanitation and sewage systems also began to cause problems. Because of a lack of capacity at the old town dump, some had begun using the abandoned mines as a site for refuse, and there were rumors that companies from other parts of the state and country also were using them as a dumping ground for industrial waste. Chemicals from this waste were leaching into the underground water table, and the old treatment plant could not effectively remove all of them from the public's water. State inspectors had twice cited city officials for failing to keep the drinking water at or above acceptable standards, but there was no increase in resources to solve this problem.

On the other hand, Tammy felt a deep sense of pride because those who remained in the community hunkered down and worked together to support one another. Just as they had during their historic battle with the coal industry, family members helped family members and friends helped friends. For example, it was not uncommon to see people visiting sick neighbors with food in hand or helping elderly residents with home repairs. Churches and civic organizations provided needy individuals with a variety of material goods such as food, clothing, household items, and shelter. Tammy knew that her community had always valued and supported its citizens, believing that people should be treated fairly and with respect.

When Tammy considered her own situation, she also experienced mixed emotions. She and her husband felt almost claustrophobic in their mobile home, which was less than one-third the size of their previous residence. It had a limited amount of property associated with it, and she was unable to grow even a modest garden of fresh vegetables. The walls were flimsy, allowing noise from their neighbors as well as from the elements to penetrate. In the winter Tammy was always too cold; in the summer she was always too hot. They had taken the best furnishings from their former home to the trailer, but this furniture had aged over the years into a dingy mess. No matter how hard Tammy tried to clean or repair items, everything in her place seemed dirty and worn. When her family or friends visited, they spent most of their time outside to avoid feeling overcrowded in the cramped living areas.

Their limited wardrobes had dwindled down to the bare necessities over time, and neither Tammy nor her husband had more than one outfit that was suitable for Sunday services, weddings, funerals, or other special occasions. They were forced to spend their own money purchasing uniforms for their jobs, and they resented the need to update these items on a regular basis. The car they had purchased when their family was younger was now a broken-down wreck with several deep dents, a faded paint job, bald tires, and engine trouble. They regularly used it to go downtown or to their jobs, but neither was willing to drive it more than a few miles at a time for safety reasons.

Money always was tight, especially around the holidays when Tammy planned special meals and purchased gifts for her family. Both she and her husband worked part-time most of the year, and their employers provided few benefits beyond a minimum-wage salary. Together they earned less than one-half her husband's previous income from the mines, and they were without medical or life insurance. Tammy prayed every day that they would continue to have good health and that their financial situation would somehow change for the better.

Her sons and daughter occasionally would give her some money, but Tammy was reluctant to accept their offers. They were struggling themselves or raising families, and Tammy felt it was her responsibility to help them rather than the other way around. In order to supplement her income from her waitress job at a fast-food restaurant, Tammy would work a second job in the sewing factory during peak periods, hoping to put away this money for special occasions.

The one saving grace was her relationships with family, friends, and neighbors. Tammy stayed in regular contact with her daughter's family, her own brothers and sisters, and her mother. As often as possible, they still had Sunday dinner together, and they continued to celebrate holidays as an extended family. It was a joyous occasion when her boys returned for a visit, and everyone came together to eat, laugh, sing, and dance. No single person or family was burdened with the expense of these get-togethers since everyone brought something they had cooked or could afford to purchase to each event.

Tammy also interacted with her friends and neighbors on a daily basis, and these relationships helped her through some very difficult times. She and her husband had known most of these people all their lives, and they were an integral part of the larger community. Borrowing food, clothing, appliances, and tools was commonplace, and no one was made to feel ashamed because of their needs. Additionally, many of these same people were members of her congregation, and they met in the church for Bible study every Wednesday evening and for regular services on

Sunday. On more than one occasion Tammy and her friends used prayer to help them deal with an illness, a death in the family, or some other tragedy.

Momma and Her Sickness

As far back as Tammy could remember, her mother had never been sick a day in her life. The kids would get all kinds of illnesses, from colds to the flu, from chicken pox to measles, but somehow Momma remained healthy. Even her father would announce from his own sickbed that this woman was immune to the ailments of mortal human beings.

When the children were ill, they received special attention from their mother that almost made feeling poorly worthwhile. They were excused from schoolwork and their chores while she nursed them back to health. She often rubbed special medicine on their chests or other affected body parts, and this attention alone made them start feeling better right away. Meals consisted of uncommon foods that held the power to heal from the inside out. Momma took time from her daily routine to sit with her sick children and read from the Bible to them or say a special prayer to Jesus asking that they feel better soon. The entire family believed in her power to heal, and they visited health-care professionals only for major problems, which occurred irregularly throughout their lives.

When Tammy's father became seriously ill with his respiratory disease, Tammy's mother went to work helping him on a full-time basis. In the beginning she made sure that he took his medicines, prepared special foods designed to alleviate his symptoms, and slowly relieved him of all responsibilities associated with maintaining their home. They were dependent upon his disability checks as their sole source of income, yet Tammy's mother found a way to pay all their regular bills as well as the extra costs for his medical care that were not covered by his health insurance. Tammy and her siblings often marveled at her ability to stretch a dollar and make the most of their limited income.

Toward the end of his life, she attended to his every need. Tammy's father was so weak physically during his last year that even breathing seemed like an impossibly difficult task for him. As a result, her mother had to wash him, dress him, clean him after his bowel movements, and help him move from room to room in their small residence. Each meal was an event in itself, and she fed him every spoonful, wiping his chin as the excess fell from his mouth. He stopped voluntarily taking his medicine, and his children believed that he was trying to hasten his own death. Nonetheless, Tammy's mother was undeterred, and she began hiding medicine in his food and feeding it to him without his knowledge.

Tammy grew to resent her father and his treatment of her mother during the final stages of his illness. She and her brothers and sisters approached their mother one afternoon, asking her how she remained so calm and cheery while confronting his sullen expression and stubbornness. Tammy would never forget how their mother scolded them for their lack of respect for and understanding of their own father. Her mother reminded them that their father was a proud and hard-working man who found it extremely difficult to be reduced to a life of dependency similar to that of an infant. In his mind he was a burden on the people he loved most in the world, and he viewed it as an intolerable situation. Regardless, their momma was duty bound to care for him lovingly until the bitter end, and the children must support her in this endeavor.

After his death Tammy's mother turned this attention to helping her family and needy people within their community. If one of her children or grandchildren or an elderly person from her church became ill, she was on the phone right away giving directions for care or advice about treatment. On many occasions Tammy or a sibling picked her up and drove her to someone's home so that she could give personal attention to an individual in need. Tammy was proud that her mother personified the community spirit that allowed her town to survive the difficult times.

One day Tammy's momma became ill and was no longer able to maintain her regular routine. It started out as a minor nuisance—a few problems associated with her coordination and movement that might have been a result of her advancing age. However, over time it matured into difficulty walking without the support of someone else and trouble focusing her eyes on objects for more than a few moments. Tammy realized it was time to do something about this problem when her mother finally seemed willing to consider medical attention.

Actually obtaining health care in their community was problematic. After the mines closed, the medical professionals employed by management were relieved of their duties and took jobs elsewhere. The only remaining clinic in town had stopped providing medical services a few years ago, and most residents survived by self-care or through the support of people like Tammy's mother. An old pharmacist still worked in the local drug store, but his ability to diagnose and treat ailments was strictly limited.

As her mother's symptoms worsened, Tammy decided that she had no choice but to take her to the closest medical office with a physician in residence. This office was located about an hour's drive from their town across treacherous mountain roads. Tammy knew that her car would never survive the trip, so she asked a neighbor if she could borrow his late-model Dodge truck. The clinic's next available appointment was a week away, and the two of them set out on the appointed day in their borrowed truck in search of professional care.

When they arrived at the clinic, Tammy was given a pile of forms to fill out concerning her mother's health status, financial situation, and insurance coverage. Tammy was embarrassed to ask her mother some of the questions on these forms, and several others confused her. She politely asked the woman behind the glass partition for some help, but this woman dismissed Tammy with the wave of a hand and told her to do the best she could on her own. Tammy returned with the incomplete forms a few minutes later, and she sat down with her mother to wait their turn.

An hour after their appointed time, her mother was ushered into one of the private rooms and Tammy was told to wait in the outer office. Tammy knew that her mother would be frightened by this separation, but she was uncomfortable challenging the orders of a woman dressed in a white medical uniform. Fifteen minutes later, her mother was shuttled back into the waiting area with a prescription in hand. When Tammy asked her what had occurred during her brief meeting with the doctor, her mother replied that he had said it was her "nerves" and that he had prescribed some nerve pills.

Tammy asked the woman behind the glass partition if she could have a moment with the doctor, but the woman quickly refused this request. The doctor was a busy man and he had already given his diagnosis to her mother. The woman noted that her mother was suffering from a form of anxiety that was common among the people who lived in this area, and the tranquilizers he had recommended should provide immediate relief. If this was not the case, they could return in a week or two and the doctor would be willing to try something else.

On the return trip Tammy became increasingly angry about the events that had occurred. They had been asked to answer difficult or impossible questions, to wait an hour for a five-minute consultation, and to believe a ridiculous explanation for her mother's troubles. Her momma was one of the strongest women Tammy had ever known, facing adversity and troublesome tasks her entire life. Why would she experience a case of nerves at this time in her life? It just didn't make sense to Tammy or her mother.

Her mother tried the pills anyway in the hope that the doctor's quick and stereotypic diagnosis might prove accurate. However, two months later her condition remained unchanged, and Tammy was truly frightened that her mother's physical health was in serious jeopardy. They decided to make a second trip to the clinic, and Tammy vowed to have the doctor listen to her mother's knowledge of her own body. They borrowed the same truck as before and returned to the medical office.

Since they had been there previously, only one new form needed to be completed. It asked the purpose of their visit, and

Tammy responded that her mother's condition had not improved as a result of the nerve pills, and they were certain that the diagnosis of anxiety was not accurate. Tammy was fearful of questioning the opinion of someone with the title "doctor," but she knew in her heart that she was right. After a forty-five-minute wait, they were both escorted into a treatment room.

When the physician arrived, he quickly examined her mother's medical chart and began providing an alternative to his previous diagnosis. He briefly described this second possibility using language that was foreign to both Tammy and her mother. Once he was satisfied with his explanation he tried to dismiss them, but Tammy insisted that he at least listen to her mother's description of what her body was telling her. He seemed irritated but agreed, attending to her story for only a few moments before cutting her off. He told them that her words only convinced him further that her problem was most likely an inner ear infection. Her mother needed to fill a new prescription that she barely could afford, and to wait and see if her condition improved. However, this treatment also failed to relieve her symptoms.

Alternative Health Care Delivery

As her mother's condition continued to deteriorate, Tammy became increasingly desperate to do something to help her. One evening while she was attending her Wednesday Bible study, a woman in her group suggested that they seek medical attention at the health mobile that visited their community once a week. Without anyplace else to turn, Tammy resolved to give it a try.

Her mother, on the other hand, was reluctant to explore this new option. The people who operated the health mobile were strangers to their community, and she was suspicious of people she didn't know coming to their town for any purpose. Why were they providing help? The rumor was that the woman in charge of dispensing health care was a Roman Catholic nun. Would she try to convert her while she administered aid? After several lengthy discussions they agreed to stop by and see for themselves what services were available.

The next visit of the health mobile was on Tuesday, and Tammy and her mother headed downtown that morning to the place where it was expected to return. There were already several people waiting patiently when they arrived, many of whom Tammy and her mother knew quite well. They openly described their experiences on their previous visits in glowing terms, relieving the newcomers of their anxieties and doubts. Tammy offered a silent prayer of thanksgiving in the belief that they might have found a way to get to the bottom of her mother's ailments.

The health mobile pulled into the town square about an hour later, and three casually dressed women emerged from the modified recreation vehicle. They cheerfully greeted the women who were in attendance, hugging those they knew from previous visits and shaking hands with the first timers. They spoke briefly with each person, trying to organize appointments according to their schedules and the severity of their conditions. Tammy's mother was given the third appointment, which was expected to take place within the next thirty minutes. If she wished, she and her daughter could come inside to wait and to have a cup of coffee.

Once inside they were struck by the colorful decor, the openness of the facility, and the informal banter between the health-care workers and the women seeking treatment. Conversations among them were rich and deep, and the women were encouraged to tell their stories in their own words, using as much time as they required. The health professionals listened intently and nodded their heads sympathetically while asking follow-up questions. Everyone was on a first-name basis, including Sister Maria, who was the head nurse practitioner. The women, patients and health-care providers alike, encouraged one another in ways that were common in this close-knit community.

When it was Momma's turn, Sister Maria asked her to sit in a comfortable chair with Tammy by her side. She began by introducing herself as a certified nurse practitioner who traveled in the health mobile from town to town throughout the area. Their services were free, but donations of money, food, and gasoline were accepted. She asked if Tammy or her mother had any questions. They had none, so the discussion of her mother's medical condition began in earnest.

Tammy's mother opened with an extensive description of her symptoms, from her first experience of them to her present state, including the lack of effectiveness of the treatments prescribed by the physician. As she continued her description, Tammy was struck by her mother's knowledge of her own body as well as the sincere interest expressed by Sister Maria. After about fifteen minutes had elapsed, the other two health-care workers were called over to listen in on their conversation. When her mother finished her lengthy talk, Sister Maria asked each of the health-care workers to give their opinions of what they had just heard. Both asked some additional questions, and they began describing possible causes using informal language. Sister Maria added her own preliminary diagnosis, and she asked Tammy's mother for her reaction.

In the end, the collaboration of patient, practitioners, and family concluded that the physician's original diagnosis of a "generalized anxiety disorder" was inaccurate. The inner ear infection was a good second choice, but the fact that her problems had continued after treatment with antibiotics suggested that it also was inaccurate. Together they agreed that a realistic possibility was some form of brain malfunction with a wide variety of causes and subsequent therapies. The next step would be a series of tests at the university-affiliated hospital that was a two-hour drive from town.

Tammy reacted to this news with some distress. She and her mother had tried to navigate the medical system previously with little success. If they couldn't get a physician in a small-town office to listen to them, how would they be able to obtain appropriate medical care in a large university hospital that was on the other side of the state? Sister Maria sympathized with their concern, but she explained that she would make the appointment with the appropriate specialist and escort them to the office. This support caused a wave of relief to wash over Tammy and her mother, and they began to feel optimistic about their future for the first time in months.

A few days later Sister Maria called to tell Tammy's mother that the testing was scheduled for the twenty-fourth of the month. This date was almost three weeks away, so Sister Maria intended to check in on Tammy's mother once a week when she passed through town. Because of logistical problems and her mother's difficulties with movement and travel, Sister Maria was willing to make a house call. Tammy's mother promised to bake one of her delicious apple pies as payment for the special treatment.

Sister Maria visited three times in the interim, staying between fifteen and thirty minutes each trip. She always greeted Tammy's mother with a friendly hug and listened to her description of how her symptoms had evolved since the last visit. Sister Maria dispensed a few medications and gave some basic medical advice each time, and they ended these sessions by saying a prayer together. Tammy wasn't sure whether it was the medicine or the prayer that helped her mother the most, but she was certain that her mother felt better following these visits.

Tammy's daughter agreed to drive them to the hospital since she had the most reliable car in the family. The three of them set out together early in the morning of the twenty-fourth, and they arrived in the college town about an hour before the appointment. They met Sister Maria in the lobby of the hospital, and she greeted them with a smile and words of encouragement. She spent the next few minutes describing the procedures Tammy's mother would undergo, their purposes, and how they might make her feel. Sister Maria promised to stay for the full two hours and answer any questions they might have along the way.

The testing proceeded as Sister Maria described, and the physicians as well as the medical technicians performing the testing were very cordial and interactive. Tammy wondered whether their deportment was due to the presence of Sister Maria, but she was thankful for it regardless. When they finished, Sister Maria and the physician in charge explained what the test results might reveal and how these results would be communicated to Tammy's mother. They agreed that it would be best for everyone concerned if Sister Maria discussed the results with them the next time she was in town. Tammy and her family returned home to wait and pray.

When Sister Maria came for her visit, Tammy, her mother, and her daughter were anxiously awaiting her arrival. She entered the mobile home with a concerned look on her face that was very telling. She proceeded to explain that the tests revealed her mother had a brain tumor that was most likely malignant and spreading to other organs in her body. Tammy's mother would have to return to the same hospital the next week so that a biopsy of the tumor could be taken. Once again, Sister Maria would be at her side, and she would help Tammy's mother make decisions about appropriate treatment. They all spent the next hour discussing possible options and planning their return trip.

The results of this second visit confirmed their worst fears, and Tammy's mother was diagnosed with a malignant form of cancer. The family sat down with Sister Maria and talked through the potential benefits and side effects of different treatment options. Tammy's mother decided that she wanted to fight her illness as aggressively as possible, and they all applauded her courage in the face of this adversity. Given the long distance to and expense of therapy at the nearest cancer care center, Sister Maria suggested that Tammy administer her mother's treatments. Sister Maria would visit every week to oversee their progress. They all agreed that this would be the best way to go.

Tammy's mother responded well to her treatments, feeling better for the first time in a long while. There was something uplifting about knowing what the real problem was and doing something about it through their efforts. Whenever Sister Maria visited, she encouraged them to remain in charge of her mother's treatment regimen and to take responsibility for her personal health and well-being.

Over the next several months the family and Sister Maria celebrated Tammy's mother's small victories over her illness and consoled one another at each setback. After six months of a variety of therapies, however, they agreed that there was nothing left they could do to fight this disease. Tammy's mother decided to live out her final days in her own home surrounded by her family and friends. Tammy remained with her twenty-four hours a day, doing everything in her power to make her mother comfortable. Sister Maria continued to visit and pray with the family during this difficult period.

What the Future Holds

As Tammy sat alongside the bed holding her mother's hand, she reflected on what things would be like without this woman's presence as a family member and a community advocate. Her mother was the matriarch of the clan—the person who brought everyone together for Sunday dinners, the holidays, and other special occasions. Even during the difficult financial period that followed the closing of the mines, she was able to marshal the resources of the collective group to make sure that no one went without food, clothing, shelter, or transportation. Sharing was a given among them, and this reciprocity helped them truly appreciate one another. Her mother made sure that they learned this important lesson well.

Tammy's mother also had done what many miners' wives must do—she nursed her husband through a debilitating illness that was a direct result of spending a career working in the coal mines. When he finally passed on, she turned this attention to her family and the needy people in her town. Even though she had little of material value to give, she gave willingly to the people who would benefit the most from it. As important, she gave her time, her advice, and herself in ways that provided comfort to others. Many people stopped by to see her during these final days, hoping to catch her awake so that they could express how much her generosity had meant to them or to a member of their family. Tammy and her kin were touched deeply by their comments and small gifts, consoling them as they prepared for her death.

Tammy realized that her life wasn't much different from her mother's. Although her husband remained in good health, the loss of his job and their precarious financial situation meant that Tammy would be required to work at menial jobs for the foreseeable future in order to survive. Her daughter was experiencing difficulties with a second pregnancy, and Tammy planned to spend as much time as possible assisting her child once her own mother passed away. Her younger son had returned home after several years in the big city, and Tammy and her husband were helping him establish a new personal and professional life in their small town.

Within the community Tammy envisioned a number of things she could do to help people thrive despite adversity. For example, she knew of many women who lived outside the town and failed to get appropriate medical care because of a variety of roadblocks. Some were too poor and were without health insurance—a common problem for people living in isolated areas of the hills. Others had some form of health insurance from the government, but they had no way of transporting themselves to a medical facility that could provide adequate health care. Tammy knew there must be a way to help these people before their illnesses progressed beyond hope—as her mother's had—and she planned on working with Sister Maria to find a workable solution.

Ultimately, Tammy recognized that she was very much like her mother. She responded to her family's needs without hesitation, coming to their aid the moment difficulties arose. Tammy was now the matriarch of her extended clan, and it would be her job to be the rallying point for all of them. She would assume responsibility for planning family events and for making sure that everyone materially, emotionally, and spiritually supported the needy among them. No one would be surprised when she adopted this role; it would be seen as a natural progression of the generations.

As Tammy looked down into the face of her mother, she couldn't help but smile. The torch had passed from mother to daughter and the exchange had been smooth. Tammy imagined that in a few years' time she would have the same reputation as her mother within their community. The situation in their town might never improve, but her family, friends, and neighbors were there to stay and they were going to do everything in their power to improve their lives. When it came to helping others, Tammy had had an excellent teacher in her mother. She hoped that her own daughter would be a willing pupil and would exercise a leadership role in their town when her time came.

SUGGESTED READINGS

This chapter was informed by:

Lee, Renee Gravois, Julie Ozanne, and Ronald Paul Hill (1999), "Improving Service Encounters through Resource Sensitivity: The Case of Health Care Delivery in Appalachia," *Journal of Public Policy and Marketing* 18 (Fall), 230–48.

Of further interest:

Duncan, Cynthia M. (1992), *Rural Poverty in America*, Westport, Conn.: Auburn House. In this volume the editor reveals that more than 9 million people living in rural areas of the United States were poor by 1990. The various chapter authors examine a broad range of the rural poor, including Appalachians in the coalfields, Native Americans on reservations, rural blacks in the South, migrant workers, and low-wage farm and manufacturing employees. The book opens with a national overview of this problem, emphasizing obstacles associated with low earnings and the working poor. The second section provides a vivid portrait of the impoverished and the communities in which they live, demonstrating how structural factors and community responses prevent escape from poverty. The third and final section discusses policies to alleviate rural poverty through empowerment strategies.

Duncan, Cynthia M. (1999), *Worlds Apart: Why Poverty Persists in Rural America*, New Haven: Yale University Press. The author of this book examines why some families and regions of the country are mired in poverty from generation to generation. In order to address this issue, 350 men and women from the Appalachian coalfields, the Mississippi Delta, and a rural New England community were interviewed over a five-year period. Results demonstrate that the impoverished in Appalachia and the Delta are socially isolated and vulnerable to a corrupt political system that divides the community into haves and have-nots. The poor are stigmatized and segregated, and lack support from schools, churches, and other civic organizations. These two communities are contrasted with the more prosperous Gray Mountain in northern New England, which avoided these same dilemmas. The volume closes with social policy recommendations that encourage mobility and build civic culture.

Gaiha, R. (1993), *Design of Poverty Alleviation Strategy in Rural Areas*, FAO Economic and Social Development Paper 115, Rome: Food and Agriculture Organization of the United Nations. This book differs from others in this bibliography in two important respects. First, it looks at rural poverty around the world rather than just within the United States. Second, it concentrates more on policy solutions and less on telling the stories of the impoverished. The author notes that the failure to alleviate global poverty in rural communities is the result of the use of inappropriate policy solutions, a limited comprehension of their impact, and poor implementation. He recommends alternative antipoverty measures that are well coordinated, financially feasible, and politically astute. Topics discussed include the measurement of poverty, government interventions, land reforms, public works projects, and collective and collaborative action.

Lyson, Thomas A., and William W. Falk (1993), *Forgotten Places: Uneven Development in Rural America*, Lawrence: University Press of Kansas. This edited book was organized by the Task Force on Persistent Rural Poverty to delve into the causes of rural impoverishment during the 1990s. The authors note that many rural regions of the United States continue to stagnate or decline despite the consistent economic growth experienced in this country after World War II. In various chapters, a lack of good jobs, poor housing conditions, and limited access to social services are described. Using a comprehensive approach, the investigation examines regions such as Central Appalachia, the black belt South, the Mississippi Delta, the Missouri Ozarks, the Lower Rio Grande Valley, the Cutover region of the upper Midwest, northern New England, the timber region of the Pacific Northwest, and rural California. The volume closes with a look at the uneven development and loss of opportunity in rural America today. Policy alternatives that improve the quality of life of rural workers and their families are provided.

SEVEN

Global Poverty
Mary and Her Land

There is a happy land,* far, far away
Where we get bread and scrape three times a day.
Bread and butter we never see
No sugar in our tea
While we are gradually
Starving away.

—Aboriginal song

While the level and amount of impoverishment in the United States is truly grave, the extent of human poverty in the entire global community is horrific. Recent research by the United Nations Development Programme reveals:

- Approximately 1.3 billion people are income poor, surviving on less than one dollar a day
- Almost 1 billion people are illiterate
- Over 1 billion people do not have access to safe drinking water
- Some 840 million people lack food security and must go hungry
- Nearly 100 million people are homeless
- About 800 million people are unable to receive health services

* That "happy land" was the Moore River Aboriginal Settlement in Western Australia.

Additional research by the UN suggests that women suffer a disproportionate share of these hardships throughout the world. For example, consumption data from North and South America, Europe, and the Commonwealth of Independent States demonstrate that female-headed households endure higher incidences of poverty than do two-parent families. In part, this inequity is a result of a wide variety of biases against women in education, employment, and asset ownership.

Aboriginal people also fare poorly. Around the world and over the course of several centuries, indigenous people have been dislocated from their original lands, herded into reserves, stripped of their cultures and ways of life, and forced into dependence upon the social welfare system. Although recent advances have been made, especially in returning land to them and empowering them to advance their economic development, indigenous people are more likely to live in poverty and to suffer a number of deprivations than are most other subpopulations.

Consistent with this profile, the focus of this chapter is on an Aboriginal woman who is a single mother. She lives with her children in a remote area of her country on a reserve near a former Catholic mission. This community suffers from high rates of alcoholism, child and spousal abuse and neglect, malnutrition, and a lack of meaningful material goods. Nonetheless, members of the community, especially the main character in this chapter, work to revive cultural traditions of language, ceremony, attachment to ancestral lands, and kinship. Over time they experience much success, but their ultimate survival as a people remains in doubt.

This story is based on original research conducted in the northwestern section of Western Australia known as the Kimberley, a vast area covering almost 450,000 square kilometers with a population of approximately 30,000 people. The focal community is several hundred kilometers by dirt roads from any major population center, and it has become a destination for the hardiest of tourists. This woman's story is one of hope in spite of years of defeat by the primary white culture that gradually permeated the entire continent.

MARY AND HER LAND

The Meaning of Land

As Mary hung up the telephone, she took a few minutes to reflect upon the conversation that had just occurred. It was her fifteenth discussion of the *Mabo* decision with a reporter or some other interested party since the recent court ruling. As the community commissioner, it was her job to answer such calls and to represent the views of her people as accurately as possible. However, Mary was becoming increasingly frustrated in this role. She shook her head, realizing that they would never really understand.

Some of the callers were hostile and antagonistic, but most were genuinely interested in comprehending the aboriginal way of life. Mary gave them credit for their sincerity. A lifetime of dealing with whitefellas, however, had convinced her that no matter how hard they tried, they were incapable of knowing the spiritual nature of the land. As she considered this situation, her eyes wandered to the window and she knew that every blade of grass, every tree, every stone that she gazed upon had a reason for being in its particular place. The land is the mother of the Aboriginal people, and they would do anything to protect it from despoliation.

At such times, her mind often rehearsed the story told to her by her grandmother and reinforced by the elders in her community about the creation of life. According to Aboriginal lore, the Creative Ancestors moved across an undifferentiated landscape during the original Dreaming in order to shape the featureless world. Each night they would sleep and dream of their activities for the following day, which would then shift from dreams to actions. In this way the Ancestors created all living things and structured the physical world.

As the Earth filled with vibrant life and natural beauty, the Ancestors tired and withdrew into every aspect of nature. Consequently Aborigines view land as a spiritual or religious phenomenon and as an extension of themselves, and they believe that their relationship to the land originated with the Dreaming. Thus, Aboriginal people assume that land rights are part of the design of the world rather than something that results from alienable legal title.

Mary learned over time that the Europeans who first came to Australia had no interest in understanding or honoring this perspective. As they spread across the continent consuming the physical resources in their paths, Aborigines were dislocated from their traditional lands to make way for white pastoralists, farmers, and miners. This dislocation caused Aboriginal people to be dislodged from their inherited culture without an opportunity to assimilate into an acceptable alternative. As a result, they experienced a series of unfamiliar systemic problems such as alcoholism, gambling addiction, poverty, and marginalization from the primary culture.

Now the *Mabo* decision was expected to make up for two centuries of domination and exploitation. Prior to this case, the courts in Australia had failed to support the historical relationship between Aborigines and the land. Based on the British doctrine of *terra nullius,* white settlers assumed that Australia was unoccupied at the time of their occupation, allowing them to ignore the indigenous people's laws and rights. However, this new ruling opened up the possibility for the first time that native title to property on the mainland of the continent might exist.

The members of Mary's community viewed this court ruling with mixed feelings. On the one hand they were excited that the land of their ancestors might revert back to its original and rightful caretakers, the Aboriginal people. As they understood the ruling, up to 50 percent of Western Australia and much of the Kimberley were Crown lands and eligible for current and future claims by Aborigines. Mary calculated that virtually all of the land of her people was available to be claimed.

She thought of her own land and the tree that her mother had dedicated to her when she was born. Over the years she and this tree had aged together, each feeling the pleasure and the pain of the other as soon as it occurred. Mary knew that when one died, the other would surely perish as well. She worried often about its safety from whites who encroached upon Aboriginal land. Mary knew that her ancestors would do everything in their power to safeguard it since their spirits remained permanently in the terrain. However, it would be a great relief if she could protect it from harm herself.

On the other hand, *Mabo* created panic in the broader white society, resulting in increased conflict between Aborigines and white Australians. A constituency made up of a variety of businesspeople and legislators was concerned that this decision would inhibit investment in at least two of the major revenue-generating industries, mining and tourism. More exaggerated concerns also existed, raising fears that Aboriginal people would sweep down from their outposts to claim the homes and yards of white people living in towns and cities.

Mary realized that such nonsense fueled negative stereotypes of her people as lazy, unreliable, and irresponsible as part of an attempt to portray them as incapable of productively owning land. Her community worried that these portraits also might be used by whitefellas to seek revenge against Aborigines by eliminating the meager support from the social welfare system which they currently received. Without the income they derived from the "dole," many Aboriginal people believed that they would be unable to survive.

Her Ancestors

Mary was fortunate in that she understood the *Mabo* decision within the context of the historical relationship between whitefellas and blackfellas. From the perspective of the Aboriginal people, there had been three distinct stages defining this relationship which evolved over time. The first stage involved annihilation of the Aboriginal people by Europeans. During this early period Aborigines were viewed as troublesome savages who roamed the land aimlessly, often stealing property from whites. Europeans were angered by their lack of awareness of and support for British law and looked upon them with disgust, believing that they had no culture, history, or religion. As a result, Aborigines either joined these invaders as second-class citizens in their own country or were eliminated or removed with brutal and lethal force.

Mary vividly remembered the stories told to her by her own ancestors, especially her grandmother and mother. Mary's grandmother had been forced off her native land when she was a child and herded with her clan onto a reserve many kilometers away. They were told that the place of their birth now belonged to the whites and that ranchers and miners would put it to productive use. This was very disconcerting to them because they treated the land with great respect and took only what they needed to survive. It was the whites who stripped the land of its natural beauty and desecrated the sites that were sacred to the Aboriginal people.

Their new home was a barren piece of property that had none of the features of their homeland. There were no streams or rivers where they could fish, and the countryside was inhospitable and desolate, almost devoid of wildlife for the men to hunt. Little of the natural habitat was edible, and the women typically returned from their gathering trips empty-handed. They had no choice but to eat the meat and produce provided by the whites, even though many of these foodstuffs were foreign to them. Taking handouts eventually eroded their ability to live independently as they slowly lost most of their incentive to use traditional means for survival.

By the time Mary's mother was born, the new policy of the whites toward Aboriginal people was that of assimilation. The goal of this stage was to absorb Aborigines into mainstream society, thereby eliminating their culture and their problems coping in the modern world. Many Aboriginal people left their homelands and moved to areas where there were high concentrations of Europeans, working in low-level service jobs or dangerous positions that few whites would assume. Children who lived on the reserves were taken from their parents and placed in residential schools to ensure that they would avoid the pitfalls of their ancestors and be better prepared for living among whitefellas. They were required to speak in English regardless of their proficiency, and they were addressed only in this language. Traditional Aboriginal practices and ceremonies were forbidden, and they were allowed to visit with family members only a few times a year.

Mary's mother recounted the story of this period in her life with a heavy heart and a deep sense of sadness. She remembered the fear and loneliness she experienced without the support and nurturing of her family, and she ran away three times, only to be returned to the school for punishment. She was lucky that she knew some English prior to her detention, but learning to think and read in English was a struggle. The clothing she was required to wear was uncomfortable and confining, and the shoes hurt her feet. Since the facility was run by a religious organization, she attended mass most days of the week and on Sundays—a ceremony that was difficult to understand because it involved another unfamiliar language.

Over the course of several years Mary's mother learned the history, religion, and culture of the whites, but she never really felt like one of them. The comments and behaviors of many of the Europeans she came in contact with suggested to her mother and her peers that they were less able and less worthy than white people were. She would never forget how white children who attended her school were segregated from black children, with the lighter-skinned Aborigines afforded somewhat better treatment and access. It was clear to her that Aboriginal people would never be accepted into the white culture as equal citizens.

Unfortunately, she began to feel less and less comfortable on her infrequent visits back home. As she aged, the Aboriginal way of life seemed foreign to her and inconsistent with her education in the mainstream culture. Furthermore, despite her love for her own people, many of the prejudices that the whites held regarding Aborigines seemed painfully accurate. Most of the people on the reserve relied entirely on government support for their livelihood and engaged in traditional practices only on an irregular basis rather than as an ongoing way of life. They lacked interest in learning white methods of education and employment but seemed infatuated with white vices such as alcohol and cigarette consumption and gambling. Mary's mother realized that she and her people were caught between cultures—unable to move forward but unable to return to the past. In the end they were dependent upon a society that vilified them and viewed them as a problem waiting for a solution.

After her schooling was complete, Mary's mother returned to the reserve to live with her family. She eventually married in a white ceremony and had several children. Mary was the youngest child in this family, and she was educated in a nearby mission school run by a group of Roman Catholic sisters. Like her mother, she learned the ways of the Europeans but failed to gain the racial status to actualize the benefits of her acculturation. Her family lived quite modestly on the reserve, dependent upon government largess to meet their basic consumption needs.

At about this time the government policy toward Aborigines shifted from assimilation to cultural renewal, with an interest in preserving what remained of the indigenous way of life. Mary's parents and other Aboriginal elders struggled to stop the disintegration of their culture through increased emphasis on their traditional ceremonies, the use of Aboriginal language, and kinship practices, but Mary and the young adults in their community were uninterested in it. As a late teen educated to believe in the superiority of white society, Mary often wondered why they held this dying culture so dear. From her perspective it only inhibited the Aboriginal people from moving forward into the twentieth century.

A Family of Her Own

By the time Mary was twenty years old, she was bored and frustrated with living on the Aboriginal reserve. She had known since birth most of the people in the community who were her age, and she experienced little excitement interacting with them. Mary had one or two close girlfriends whom she relied upon for emotional support, and they often fantasized together about life in a big city. Through an assortment of magazines, movies, records, and books, they imagined the outside world as containing a treasure-trove of material possessions too numerous to comprehend. Fancy cars, beautiful and stylish clothing, gourmet foods, and homes with elaborate furnishings and luxurious lawns and gardens filled their thoughts and caused them to ache with desire. Though they had never visited such places, they were certain that more opportunity to acquire goods existed there than the relative poverty of Aboriginal life in a remote location could provide.

One of the few meaningful distractions for Mary and some of the other young women were the white male workers who performed a variety of functions on Aboriginal land. Included in this category were skilled craftsmen who supported the community through carpentry, plumbing, and electrical and mechanical work. They often came from faraway places and brought the trappings of city life with them. Some were quiet, others friendly, but virtually all of them showed interest in the single Aboriginal women. Mary received more than her share of attention from them because of her attractive features and slim figure, her modest European wardrobe, which she had pieced together over time, and her outgoing nature and curiosity to learn more about white Australia.

An encounter with a particular young man blossomed into a full-blown romance for Mary. He was about ten years her senior and had come up North several years before to ply his trade. He worked in many Aboriginal communities during this time, taking occasional trips back to Perth to visit his family. He made Mary feel special and attractive despite her being an Aborigine, and he promised to take her to visit a big city on his next holiday. Mary grew to love him through these encounters, and they decided to wed as soon as possible.

Mary's parents, however, were very resistant to the idea. They were certain that any marriage between whites and blacks was doomed to failure, and they recounted stories to her of several disastrous biracial marriages within the community which had occurred over the years. Her parents believed that the cultural differences between whitefellas and blackfellas were too great to overcome, even within a union of two people who were very much in love. They also felt that white Australians would never completely accept their daughter or any subsequent children, leaving them as second-class citizens. It was their opinion that Mary should remain at home with them until an appropriate Aboriginal suitor could be found.

Mary and this man decided to ignore her parents' warnings and marry without their consent. She knew this decision would deeply hurt her parents, but Mary was ready to trade the squalor of their Aboriginal community for the material trappings of life among whites. They decided that the best solution was to elope without telling anyone and to get married in the town of Geraldton. Mary carefully packed her clothing and a few pictures of her family and friends in preparation for their journey. She was thrilled and frightened at the same time. Mary realized that she finally would see the places and things that she had dreamed about for the last several years. With her fiancé's income potential and savings, they should be able to afford to purchase new clothing, a recent-model car, and a nicely furnished home. However, Mary was apprehensive about how his family and friends, as well as white people in general, would treat her. If her parents' concerns materialized, she would forever remain an outsider.

Mary put the negative thoughts out of her mind and concentrated on the positive possibilities. Australian society had come a long way since the annihilation and assimilation policies of the past, and she believed that her education in the mission school had prepared her for living in a white city. The more she thought about it, the more certain she was about her decision. Her children would thank her someday for letting them grow up as whites instead of as Aborigines.

Leaving and Coming Home

Mary eventually wed this man, but it was without the blessing of his family as well. His parents had many of the same concerns as her parents, but the young couple chose to ignore this second opinion. To them, it was their relationship and dedication to each other that truly mattered. Their families failed to understand that this essential ingredient would ensure their long-term success. They married in a brief ceremony and settled down to live their lives.

Over the next few years they had two children, a son and a daughter. They lived together as a family in a modest two-bedroom house in a suburban area of a midsize city. It was sparsely but tastefully furnished in a traditional middle-class fashion, and Mary was pleased with how each room came together with the same theme. Mary and her husband shared use of a new Ford sedan that they purchased—an automobile that was nicer than anything available in her Aboriginal community. They traveled regularly to a variety of places in Western Australia, and they took an annual vacation to a coastal resort area several hundred kilometers away.

The first decade of their marriage seemed to pass with lightning speed for Mary. In the beginning she invested all her time and energy into making their home a special place for them to live. Once this task was accomplished her children were born, and she spent the next phase of their union nurturing and attending to them. Mary did everything in her power to prepare them for life in a white community through their dress, deportment, and understanding of the broader culture. She was pleased with their development and certain that they would blend nicely with the other children when the time came for their formal schooling.

Unfortunately, her children did experience some of the prejudice that her parents had predicted. Once in school they performed well as students and were outgoing, but they received few invitations to visit the homes of their peers or to attend special events such as birthday parties. Her children often pleaded with her to intervene on their behalf, and Mary did call some of the mothers of their schoolmates to arrange play dates. Occasionally one would agree to get together, but these mothers rarely reciprocated with an invitation to their homes. Most of the time they made flimsy excuses and tried to get off the phone as quickly as possible. Mary also approached several of these parents at various school functions to assure them that their children were safe in her home. They usually responded politely but then excused themselves after a few minutes of stilted conversation.

After fifteen years of living in this community, Mary began experiencing bouts of depression. By this time she had all the material possessions she had desired during her youth, but these things no longer were enough to sustain her sense of self. The house, car, and clothes seemed more of a bother than a source of joy or excitement. She had worked so hard to accumulate such property only to find out that it was meaningless to her. She also began to feel as if her identity as a human being were slipping away. She had relished the roles of wife and mother, but the sense of fulfillment she had experienced previously was rapidly dissipating. Mary felt as if she had somehow lost her way, without a clear direction for the future.

It was during this period that she realized her persona as an Aborigine had eroded over time. She also recognized that this loss was her own fault. Mary had become "a stranger in a strange land," doing everything in her power to ignore her heritage while failing to become a member of the dominant white culture. She had raised her children to operate the same way, and they had succeeded in having few of the traits, attitudes, and behavior patterns of Aboriginal children. For example, they knew little about their land, ancestors, and the culture of their people. Over the years they had visited the reserve only twice—both times to bury relatives. They quickly tired of the community on these visits, wanting to return home to their middle-class white way of life as soon as possible.

During this same period, her siblings informed Mary that their mother had passed away suddenly of an unknown illness.

The news sent her into a panic, and she gathered up her children and returned to her homeland for the funeral. After driving virtually nonstop for two days they arrived just in time for the ceremony, which was a mixture of European and Aboriginal rituals that seemed odd when performed together. After all the events had concluded, Mary and the children retired to her mother's house for a night's sleep before their return trip home on the following day.

During her restless sleep the spirits of her mother and grandmother presented Mary with a singular message: their community was in trouble and Mary was the only person who could help them. They acknowledged that her identity as an Aboriginal person was receding, and they explained that her loss was symbolic of the disintegration of Aboriginal culture within the larger community. Now that the trappings of white culture such as television, movies, and music were so readily available, the younger generation was becoming increasingly uninterested in Aboriginal culture and the sacred nature of their land. Many of the men preferred to drink and gamble, and these European ills were now affecting some of the women as well. Unless Mary did something soon to save their community, their culture would surely perish. It would be a difficult task to accomplish, but they were committed to helping her along the way.

When Mary awoke the next morning, she resolved to stay in her homeland and do everything in her power to help her community. She told her children of this decision during breakfast, and they immediately protested with a barrage of anxious questions. Where would they live? Surely not in their grandmother's hovel, which had few of the comforts of their middle-class home. What about their friends back home? The Aboriginal children in this community were a poor replacement and seemed very foreign to them. Finally, would they be separated permanently from their father? They were certain that he would never give up his life in the city and return to this Aboriginal town.

Mary calmly responded to all of their concerns by telling them not to worry. It was her duty to return to her people at this critical juncture in order to help them renew their identity as Aborigines. Her mother and grandmother would protect them from harm and assist them in getting reacquainted with their people. The children had no understanding of what it meant to be an Aboriginal person, and they needed to learn the value of their ancestors' ways before it was too late. They would make new friends who would help them in this process, and they were old enough to support their mother as she came to the aid of her community. Mary hoped that her husband would agree to join them, but she would stay regardless of his intentions or actions. The responsibility given to her by the maternal side of her family was a sacred charge that she could not ignore.

Losing Ground

The events of the next year would test Mary's resolve in every possible way. Her husband never joined them in the Aboriginal community; instead he began a new life for himself with a white woman he had known most of his adult life. Her children refused to acclimate to their surroundings, preferring to soak up as many European goods and services as were available on the reserve. In fact, they seemed to enjoy their status as outsiders from a white city, and they spent much of their day introducing their peers to the dress, mannerisms, and style of their previous life. Mary wondered whether their actions were a form of teenage rebellion or a response to the threat to their identity as (part) white people. Either way, their behaviors were at cross-purposes with Mary's intentions.

The community's reaction to Mary's early leadership attempts was mixed at best. The children seemed more interested in her experiences in white cities than they were in learning about their own culture. The women were confused and frightened by another woman who exhibited so much command and publicly expressed so many strong opinions. They would never have had the desire or ability to do so in front of their men, and they decided to hold back from joining her until the adult males in their community expressed approval.

The men were another story altogether. Most had grown up on the reserve with few opportunities for personal and professional development, and they were dependent upon government handouts for their livelihood. Their understanding of the traditional role of men in an Aboriginal community was a faint memory of an era that existed before their time. Few actively followed the ways of their ancestors since these activities were no longer necessary for their survival. Instead, they often spent their time playing cards and drinking beer. What little remained of their welfare checks when these consumption rituals were completed provided for their families' needs.

As a result, their wives and children often lived in squalor and in fear for their long-term safety. For example, most families inhabited three-room shacks made of corrugated steel which baked in the hot sun of summer and were near freezing during the most severe winter weather. When the rainy season arrived, the roofs leaked in so many places that no one bothered to try to contain the flow of water. The winds that accompanied these rains whipped through the houses as if the walls didn't exist at all. Pets and assorted livestock wandered in and out of their homes at will, eating bits of food that had fallen to the floor. The debris from a thousand meals accumulated in the kitchen area. Rooms were dusty and dirty in the dry weather and wet and muddy when it rained. Electricity from the community generator was sporadic at best, and it powered a precious few basic appliances such as refrigerators, televisions, and lights.

Since most families lacked the ability or desire to acquire their own food using traditional Aboriginal methods, they were dependent upon the local community store, which sold a variety of foodstuffs. Fresh produce and meats were hard to come by in such a desolate area, and the owners relied upon a weekly delivery of goods from down south to replenish their stock. Thus, milk, eggs, fruits, and vegetables were typically in short supply or of poor quality and expensive to purchase. Most families substituted for these staples with a variety of less costly canned goods, which lacked the nutritional value of the items they replaced. Mary noticed that the children, in particular, made poor food choices when they had an opportunity to select their own purchases, preferring candy and soda to more healthful alternatives. In fact, regardless of age, the top-selling nonalcoholic beverage in their community was Coca-Cola.

The provision of health care was equally inadequate. A community health nurse stopped by to attend to the people's needs once or twice a month, but she could do little more than treat their problems in a superficial manner in the time she had available. With the high incidence of drinking and smoking in the community, the physical condition of most of the men and women over age forty was quite poor. The nurse often recommended changes in their consumption habits and physical routines, but few adults listened. Additionally, the children suffered from a number of nutritional deficiencies because of their restricted diets, and many of them had rotting teeth because of the high refined-sugar content of their primary foodstuffs and poor oral hygiene. The nurse again recommended dietary changes as well as vitamin supplements, but most children ignored her advice and had some of their teeth removed annually when the university dental school students visited.

Mental health within the community also was suffering. Each day a large group of men would gather at the liquor store by 8:00 A.M., waiting for it to open for business. One by one they would go inside and use their welfare dollars to purchase a carton (case) of beer for their personal consumption. They would then sit together in the corner of a wooded area and drink until all their communal beer was gone. Drunk and unhappy to be without additional liquor, they would return home to their families. At such times, they might express their irrational anger and take out their frustrations on innocent family members, resulting in widespread spousal and child abuse.

They themselves and their victims rarely held the men responsible for such aberrant behavior—the whole community blamed it on the "grog." Thus, such men were without remorse for their destructive actions after they sobered up and were in denial about their alcoholism. Mary felt certain that some of this acting out was due to the loss of their traditional role as men. Yet it didn't justify their behavior. Mary worried that more and more of the women were joining these men during their binges rather than seeking a more healthful solution.

Now that she viewed her community through mature eyes, Mary understood why so many young adults chose to leave the reserve when the opportunity presented itself. The role of the adult male had been reduced from the traditional one of the patriarch of the clan, who used his skills to nourish and nurture his family, to that of an unemployed dependent, who often squandered his family's resources. The life of an adult female was equally tragic. She spent her days in hopeless dependence on such a man, without the ability to acquire the things necessary to raise her children in a healthful and developmental environment. Any children born to such a union seemed destined to live in poverty, to suffer physically and emotionally, and to repeat the same cycle when they became adults.

After years of education in the mission or government schools, these young people had a vision of the larger world as a place of greater opportunity and promise than the Aboriginal community could ever provide. As their traditional culture lapsed into disregard and disrepair, it had slowly been replaced by the material white culture that was revered in the media. The movies, television programs, and music that the young people eagerly watched and listened to introduced them to a world of consumption and ideas that they could only dream about in such a desolate area.

Mary knew that they had one foot in the world of blackfellas and one foot in the world of whitefellas, and they were eager, as young people often are, to move forward and get their fair share of the world's resources. However, Mary also knew that leaving their community would never fulfill their dreams. Their education would always be inferior to that provided in white communities, and, unless they had unique and highly sought-after talents, in sports or music, for example, they would never be accepted completely by the primary white culture. Although leaving the reserve seemed like the only solution, her experience demonstrated that running away would not satisfy their desires in the long run. Instead, they needed to learn how to be true Aboriginal people living in a white society.

Seeking a Compromise

Mary was nearly overwhelmed by the difficulties facing her community and by the challenges they had to overcome to resolve those difficulties. They needed to find a way to instill a renewed sense of pride in themselves, their land, and Aboriginal customs and traditions in general. Once this difficult task was accomplished, the community could turn its attention to solving its physical and mental health problems, replacing poor habits and behaviors with healthier ways of living that would provide real meaning to their lives. Of course they could never return to the days before the white invasion. However, they had to seek and find a compromise that would blend Aboriginal and European cultures in ways consistent with building a positive future for the men and women in their community on their own terms.

Mary realized that the only way she could have the necessary impact would be to seek and obtain a formal position of authority within the reserve. Joining the Council of Elders was one possibility, but Mary was afraid that she would become a lone voice among the throng of entrenched elders who would defend the status quo. Instead she decided to run for the only elective office in the community, the job of community commissioner. The person who occupied this position was the liaison between the outside world and their community, making a host of decisions about the use of government money. Additionally, the commissioner enforced the rules and regulations of the reserve as well as the state, and he or she represented the Aboriginal people before white constituencies and other indigenous groups.

Mary started her campaign without announcing it to anyone. She worked tirelessly for the children of the community as an advocate at the local school, as an aide with the public health nurse, and as an organizer of sports and other events at the community center. Once the children accepted her unconditionally, the men in the community gave their approval and the women joined her in these activities as well as others. For example, Mary and the other women started a program to clean up the grounds within the reserve and mend some of the older homes that were in disrepair. After several initial successes, a few of the men allied themselves with them, signaling a level of acceptance for Mary and her activities which no woman had ever achieved. She ran unopposed for the commissioner's position in the next election and began a three-year term.

Her first order of business was to re-engage members of the community with their cultural heritage. Mary started weekly events where the community elders discussed or performed traditional dances or ceremonies with the young people in the reserve. Over time these events evolved into a series of field trips to places that represented sacred sites to Aborigines. Mary was surprised at how many young people showed up for these excursions and how little they actually knew about the meaning of land to their people. The next step involved offering formal classes in their native language. Several of the older women got together to develop visual aids to help the children understand the meaning behind each of the words. The community elders remarked with pride that they could hear their native tongue spoken widely within the reserve for the first time in recent memory.

The health issues were thorny problems, and Mary decided to tackle them one at a time. She recognized that they would never have a full-time physician, nurse, or dentist in their community, so it was up to them to take charge of their own health. To this end, Mary worked with the local store to broaden its offerings to include healthier alternatives. Additionally, she involved the elders by having them teach young people how to hunt, fish, and otherwise seek food using traditional Aboriginal methods so that they could supplement their diets with lean meats and fresh produce. In order to instill a sense of community with regard to these activities, Mary made sure that each party of hunters and gatherers was given a big sendoff by their kin and that they returned to a hearty welcome home. The foods often were prepared and consumed communally, further enhancing Aboriginal self-respect and independence.

The problem of alcoholism within the community was the most difficult to resolve. Aborigines had only recently been granted legal access to liquor, but it had been a problem since the arrival of Europeans. Few among them knew how to limit consumption, and they exonerated themselves for their destructive behaviors while under alcohol's influence. Mary knew that she must convince the community that drinking in moderation was acceptable and that abusive behavior while intoxicated would not be tolerated.

Several community meetings on this issue took place without a final resolution. At the next meeting, Mary came prepared with a list of those dead, severely ill, or injured over the last few years as a result of alcohol consumption, and the community sat in stunned silence as she read their names. By the close of the meeting, the community decided to limit the amount of alcohol for all adults to a specified number of cans per week, and to keep the liquor store open only in the afternoons. It wasn't a perfect solution, but Mary felt it was a good start.

The final phase of her appointment as commissioner was spent reducing the community's dependence upon the social welfare system. Mary recognized that no one is free who lives from month to month on government handouts. Additionally, this dependence saps initiative, limits opportunities, and adversely affects self-esteem. However, there were no profitable enterprises within the reserve except the local food and liquor stores, and Mary knew that these retail establishments could employ only a handful of Aborigines at the most basic of jobs. What they needed were new enterprises that allowed a broad segment of the community to blend their cultural gifts with the white entrepreneurial spirit. The dilemma that they faced was how to actualize this unique combination of traditional and modern approaches to work.

Mary decided to seek the help of the state-run economic development organization to find the right path. Together they discovered that many of the Aboriginal elders had artistic talents that they hadn't practiced in years. With the provision of Aboriginal as well as European materials, they were able to create some beautiful artifacts that mirrored the artistry of their ancestors. An art dealer from down south took many of these items on consignment, and the first Aboriginal-run business in their community was begun. Over time several of the younger Aborigines joined in after discovering their own artistic talents and abilities.

Other community members began a variety of businesses of their own, including the development of a tourist trade on their land for the first time. A group of the men built a series of Aboriginal-style dwellings, and they worked with a travel office in Perth to market this as a way to experience an ancient mode of life. It began with a trickle of hardy travelers who slept in the huts, traveled to sacred sites to hear the stories of the ancestors, and hunted and ate the meat from their kills. This business grew rapidly, but the community elders decided to limit its growth in order not to disrupt the flow of life within the reserve.

Survival of the Fittest

At the end of her three-year term, Mary decided not to seek a second appointment as community commissioner. Over time several of the men in the community had grown uncomfortable with her influence and power within the reserve, and they planned to support a man of their choice for the position. Additionally, a small group of women were jealous of her status and vowed to put their own candidate on the ballot. Mary surmised that politics were the same no matter where you lived.

In any case, Mary recognized that it was time for her to step aside. She had worked tirelessly to improve conditions within her community and to create an environment that instilled in community members a renewed sense of pride in their status as Aboriginal people. Things had changed significantly, and she knew that her activities had been the catalyst. Mary had accomplished everything she had set out to do, and she had fulfilled the pledge to her mother and grandmother which she had made following their visit to her in a dream. It was now time for someone else to provide leadership and continue the work of cultural revival.

One of the few criticisms of her tenure as commissioner that Mary took to heart involved the hybrid nature of culture that resulted from her work. These critics applauded the return of traditional Aboriginal activities and language, but they felt these changes did not go far enough. Their goal was to remove all things European from their lives, including electricity and the appliances it ran, automobiles, telephones, processed foodstuffs and alcohol, and the whites who worked in the community. They were particularly interested in stopping the barrage of media—especially television, movies, and music. From their perspective, these goods, influences, and people had caused the cultural disintegration in the first place, and their removal would eliminate temptations from the younger generation of Aborigines.

While Mary sympathized with their intentions, she knew these critics would never reach their goal of eliminating the influence of white society. It was too pervasive and powerful for a small community such as theirs to contain. It promised a world of material possessions which would always be attractive to young people—a world that the Aboriginal community could never promise or provide. It would implicitly tell them that they failed to measure up, and it would beckon them to leave their homeland. Unfortunately, it would never make good on its promise of material reward for turning away from Aboriginal culture. Their education, socialization, and the color of their skin would be used against these young people, and they would forever exist outside the mainstream.

From Mary's viewpoint, the larger dilemma was one of cultural survival. While the community was in a better place than it had been a few years ago, the same external forces continued to exert pressure, and the people remained dependent upon the government for the bulk of their revenue. They were a small people with modest personal resources in a continuing battle with the primary white society. They had won this last skirmish, but the war was far from over. Their relative poverty and deprivation left them without the means to elevate their status within the larger society on a permanent basis. In Mary's mind the real issue was how much of their original culture would remain as they sought a protected place in the white world. The culture of the Aborigines may be 150,000 years old. Would it continue to endure in the new millennium?

SUGGESTED READINGS

This chapter was informed by:

Hill, Ronald Paul, (1995), "Blackfellas and Whitefellas: Aboriginal Land Right, the *Mabo* Decision, and the Meaning of Land," *Human Rights Quarterly* 17 (May), 303–22.

Hill, Ronald Paul, and Bahram Adrangi (1999), "Poverty and the United Nations," *Journal of Public Policy and Marketing* 18 (fall), 135–46.

Hill, Ronald Paul, and Kanwalroop Kathy Dhanda (1999), "Gender Inequity and Quality of Life: A Macromarketing Perspective," *Journal of Macromarketing* 19 (December), 140–52.

Of further interest:

Chossudovsky, Michel (1997), *The Globalisation of Poverty: Impacts of IMF and World Bank Reforms,* London: Zed Books Ltd. This book is premised on the belief that much poverty results from global debt collection that ultimately destroys jobs and hinders economic activity. The author notes that external debt has reached $2 trillion in the developing world, resulting in currency destabilization and subsequent social strife, ethnic conflicts, and civil war. This debt crisis has resulted in macroeconomic policies by the International Monetary Fund (IMF) and World Bank which caused state institutions to collapse, economic borders to be eliminated, and millions of people to become impoverished. The first part of the book concentrates on global poverty and macroeconomic reform. Part 2 focuses attention on sub-Saharan Africa, historically one of the most poverty-stricken regions of the world. Part 3 looks at South and Southeast Asia, with special attention given to Bangladesh and Vietnam. Part 4 concentrates on Latin America, and part 5 discusses the former Soviet Union and the Balkans.

Hunter, Ernest (1993), *Aboriginal Health and History: Power and Prejudice in Remote Australia*, Melbourne, Victoria: Cambridge University Press. This book differs from others in this bibliography in that it focuses on the area of the world where the original research described earlier took place: the Kimberley in Western Australia. The author demonstrates how social disruption by white Europeans on the continent resulted in cultural dislocation and loss of power by Aboriginal people. Using an intercultural context, the author discusses rising Aboriginal mortality rates from suicide, homicide, and accidents. Additionally, the role of alcohol consumption among Aborigines is discussed, with an emphasis on its effect on violence to self and others, mental and physical health, and the economy. Dislocation and the loss of economic benefits derived from the Aborigines' traditional lands exacerbate their problems.

United Nations Development Programme (1997), *Human Development Report 1997*, New York: Oxford University Press. This volume posits the eradication of poverty as a worldwide goal that should be at the forefront of international politics following the end of the Cold War. Poverty is defined as more than low income and includes issues related to health, education, freedom, dignity, and self-respect. To this end, the *Report* advances the Human Poverty Index as an appropriate measure; it is composed of variables associated with survival, knowledge, and standard of living. The volume closes with six recommendations for eradicating poverty worldwide: empowering individuals, households, and communities; strengthening gender equality; accelerating pro-poor growth; improving the management of globalization; ensuring an active state or government; and taking special actions for special situations.

United Nations Development Programme (1997), *Human Development Papers 1997: Poverty and Human Development*, New York: United Nations Publications. The articles in this book examine a number of issues related to global poverty. The first chapter looks at the relationship between human development and poverty, a topic often discussed in UN publications. The second chapter concentrates on globalization and how it has generated inequality in economic growth and poverty across nations. The third chapter examines the oft-overlooked area within the study of global poverty of problems in advanced industrial nations. The fourth chapter tackles the knotty problem of poverty measurement and definition using an approach that is consistent with the HPI discussed in the volume noted previously. The fifth chapter focuses on empowerment, a solution that also is consistent with the 1997 *Report*. The book closes with a final chapter that once again directs attention to poverty in developed nations.

EIGHT

A Closing Look at Poverty

A Chilly, blustery day in Dixie,
overcast skies, sleet, freezing rain;
no more room in the city shelters
as the Dow scales 7000 for the first time.

Kids selling their bodies in the ghetto,
crack addicted mothers oblivious to pain,
another shooting in the projects
as the Dow scales 7000 for the first time.

Starving people in Sub-Saharan Africa,
abject poverty in South Asia,
Taliban imprisoning women in homes
as the Dow scales 7000 for the first time.
                        —Vimal, "Dow Jones"

Surviving in a Material World

Taken together, the short stories in this volume provide a vivid portrait of what it is like to live in our material world without adequate access to the wide variety of goods and services available to typical middle-class consumers. From the homeless who exist outside the social welfare system to those who live in municipal

161

and private shelters, and from the welfare families whose primary source of income is government handouts to Aborigines who live on the dole, these people share several important characteristics. First, they face severe restrictions in their ability to meet basic consumption needs. Second, they are excluded from mainstream society and the decision-making processes that affect their material lives. Third, they successfully cope with these restrictions and exclusions using strategies and sources of strength that often prove to be surprisingly resourceful.

This book includes several examples of individuals and families who were unable to meet their most fundamental material needs. For instance, both Jack and Zoë eventually were without adequate shelter after exhausting opportunities to stay with family and friends. Jack ultimately ended up living in an abandoned building, and Zoë and her family eventually lived in a private shelter run by a Catholic religious community. Additionally, Zoë and Anita faced difficulties providing healthy food for their families. As a result they often relied on less nutritious alternatives such as fast food and inexpensive substitutes such as Kool-Aid. Finally, Tammy and her mother were unable to locate appropriate medical care within a reasonable distance of their town. Instead they had to travel several hours over treacherous mountain roads to have their critical needs met.

All of the people whose lives are chronicled in these stories faced social deprivation and exclusion from the decisions that affected their lives. Consider Jack and Mary. Because of Jack's physical appearance and mannerisms and because of the color of Mary's skin and her Aboriginal heritage, most of the people they came in contact with in the primary culture avoided, ignored, or disparaged them. Eddie and Anita's children found that the bright light of their childhood was extinguished when they were deprived of the material abundance displayed by the media. Finally, Zoë, Anita, and Tammy regularly interacted with private and public service personnel who sought little or no input when making decisions that dramatically affected their material lives.

Nonetheless, despite these adversities the focal characters in these stories persevered. While they lacked economic and cultural capital that might have translated into power, prestige, and affluence, they sought out social capital in the form of community, which ultimately provided them with a source of strength and resilience. For example, Mary worked within her Aboriginal reserve to instill pride among her people in their ancient culture and to find traditional ways of life that would allow them to become more independent and self-reliant. Both Tammy and Anita sought leadership roles in their local church groups in order to marshal the limited resources of their town or neighborhood in support of those in need. Even Jack was able to improve his housing arrangements by living with or near other homeless people. In fact, it was the lack of community support and the opportunities it provides that left Zoë and her children with no place to live and Eddie without an alternative to a life of crime.

Poverty Eradication in the Twenty-first Century

Beginning with the *Universal Declaration of Human Rights*, which was adopted by the United Nations General Assembly on December 10, 1948, freedom from poverty and its negative repercussions acquired the status of a basic human right alongside civil and political rights. Over the last two decades several additional global pronouncements have advanced this cause, with special attention given to vulnerable groups such as women and children. Culminating in the *Copenhagen Declaration on Social Development* in 1995, which argued that a post-Cold War society should make the eradication of poverty a priority, 1996 was designated the International Year for the Eradication of Poverty and the period 1997–2006 as the United Nations Decade for the Eradication of Poverty.

Such political pronouncements follow ethical imperatives advanced by leading scholars such as John Rawls of Harvard University. His theory of distributive justice, titled Justice as Fairness, is based on the belief that social and economic inequalities are just only if they are to the advantage of all members of society, especially the least advantaged or the poor. However, in a world where the richest 20 percent in the global economy control 86 percent of the wealth, while the poorest 20 percent control little more than 1 percent, the situation clearly is unjust. In fact, the ratio of the incomes of the richest 20 percent to those of the poorest 20 percent has increased from 30 to 1 in 1960 to 78 to 1 by the mid-1990s, demonstrating that injustice is on the rise.

While this volume does not explicitly discuss poverty as a human rights violation, it should be clear to the reader that the focal characters in these stories, as well as their families and their communities, face restrictions that unnecessarily reduce the quality of their lives. These restrictions suggest the potential violation of economic and social rights, including:

- The right to basic goods and services
- The right to human dignity and self-respect
- The right to participate in society in a meaningful way
- The right to a living wage
- The right to a positive future

Each of these rights is discussed in turn.

The right to security in the provision of basic goods and services is fundamental to all other rights because without their availability a person is consumed with the need to acquire them. For example, consider the amount of energy and time that went into seeking or constructing basic shelter by Zoë and Jack, or the activity required by Tammy to get a proper diagnosis and treatment of her mother's illness. The subpopulations of people who informed these short stories spend a much greater portion of their day in search of essential commodities than do their middle-class counterparts. Societies and governments typically agree on little when it comes to the poor, but it is time that the world community set a universal standard for the unconditional provision of food, shelter, health care, and clothing to all human beings.

Once these basic needs are met and their future provision is secure, attention can turn to the right to human dignity and self-respect. All people should be afforded a certain level of status by virtue of their membership in the human family without regard to color, gender, location, or income level. As a global society, we need to promote public understanding of the complexity, diversity, and difficulty of the material lives of the impoverished as well as their tenacity in solving their own problems. Internal empowerment, through community-based organizations and methods that raise awareness among the impoverished of their resource strengths and weaknesses, can help them cope with their life circumstances and learn how to work effectively together. The stories involving Anita and Tammy provide good examples of internal empowerment, especially among groups of women.

The right to participate in society in a meaningful way follows quickly on the heels of the previous right. Both Jack and Mary became so alienated from the primary culture that they dropped out and found alternative living styles. Anita ended up so frustrated with the social welfare system and its lack of flexibility or concern for how well it served her family's needs that she eventually subverted the system in order to survive. If societies eventually understand the true material existence of the poor, we may begin to recognize the provision of a basic package of goods and services as a public entitlement rather than a public nuisance. Regardless, poverty communities need to evolve their sources of internal empowerment for external use in order to influence their public persona and gain the political clout necessary to direct their futures.

The right to a living wage requires that governments, working together with private industry, establish a package of pay and benefits for full-time workers at the lower end of the socioeconomic scale which allows a family to meet its primary consumer needs. Such a package is essential given the recent reform movement of welfare-to-work which affects the lives of millions of American families. As the story of Anita suggests, the ability of these families to leave the social welfare system successfully requires an acceptable occupation to take its place. Events following recent increases in the minimum wage in the United States have proved that pessimistic outlooks predicting job losses were wrong. In truth, a healthy global economy with increasing productivity has considerable room to expand wage rates at the lower end. A set of services deemed necessary to long-term success such as medical and child care benefits should round out this package.

The right to a positive future completes the list and ensures that current poverty conditions are no longer a self-fulfilling prophesy. As information- and technology-based employment replaces the unionized jobs held by people like the men in the lives of Zoë, Anita, and Tammy, our society needs to make sure that the least advantaged are not left behind. Community-based programs that involve continuous training and lifetime learning among adults may provide the opportunity necessary for people to rise out of poverty or avoid it altogether. Such programs could be attached to the local schools where teachers and administrators accept a broader perspective of the constituency they serve. Of course, success depends upon parity of the school systems in impoverished neighborhoods with those in more affluent areas so that the next generation will have the educational skills necessary to compete successfully for college placement or positions in the job market.

Closing Thoughts

While the reader may endorse some or all of these rights, their provision might appear prohibitively expensive, especially on a worldwide basis. However, in a global economy of approximately $25 trillion, the financial resources necessary to eliminate poverty currently exist. The United Nations estimates the price tag for providing universal access to essential goods and services (such as health care, nutrition, safe drinking water, and education) and for providing monetary transfers to abolish income poverty at

$80 billion annually. This amount is less than 0.5 percent of the world's income, or the net worth of the seven richest people on the planet.

One proposal to help pay for meeting the goal of poverty eradication in the twenty-first century is the 20:20 Initiative. First advanced by the United Nations Development Programme in its *Human Development Report 1992,* and endorsed by the World Summit in Copenhagen three years later, this proposal recommends that governments allocate 20 percent of their budgets to funding a baseline package of goods and services for all citizens. The same proposal asks that donor countries dedicate an equivalent percentage of their aid budgets to the provision of universal coverage, regardless of their political agendas.

Nonetheless, money alone will not be enough. A universal standard of living may prolong the lives of the impoverished, but it does not guarantee a better quality of life. In a world where the poor are segregated from mainstream society, vilified or misrepresented by politicians, and ignored or mistreated by those who control the provision of basic goods and services, their lives will continue to be characterized by humiliation, alienation, anxiety, and rage. I hope the stories in this book help the reader go beyond the negative stereotypes that portray the poor as unworthy of our respect or support. Ultimately, when we remove our middle-class lenses of affluence and opportunity and replace them with lenses of poverty and restriction, our understanding of how and why people become or remain impoverished is forever changed.

Bibliography

Allan, Emilie Anderson, and Darrell J. Steffensmeier (1989), "Youth Underemployment and Property Crime: Differential Effects of Job Availability and Job Quality on Juvenile and Young Adult Arrest Rates," *American Sociological Review* 54 (February), 107–23.

Alwitt, Linda F., and Thomas D. Donley (1997), "Retail Stores in Poor Urban Neighborhoods," *Journal of Consumer Affairs* 31 (Summer), 139–64.

Andreasen, Alan R. (1975), *The Disadvantaged Consumer*, New York: The Free Press.

Baker, Susan Gonzalez (1994), "Gender, Ethnicity, and Homelessness," *American Behavioral Scientist* 37 (February), 476–504.

Beaver, Patricia Duane (1986), *Rural Community in the Appalachian South*, Prospect Heights, Ill.: Waveland Press.

Belk, Russell W. (1988), "Possessions and the Extended Self," *Journal of Consumer Research* 15 (September), 139–68.

Bell, Judith, and Bonnie Maria Burlin (1993), "In Urban Areas: Many of the Poor Still Pay More for Food," *Journal of Public Policy and Marketing* 12 (Fall), 260–70.

Blank, Rebecca (1989), "The Effect of Medical Need and Medicaid on AFDC Participation," *Journal of Human Resources* 24 (Winter), 54–87.

——— (1997), *It Takes a Nation: A New Agenda for Fighting Poverty*, Princeton: Princeton University Press.

Blank, Rebecca, and Patricia Ruggles (1994), "Short-Term Recidivism among Public Assistance Recipients," *American Economic Review* 84 (2), 49–53.

Blau, Joel (1988), "On the Uses of Homelessness: A Literature Review," *Catalyst* 22, 5–25.

Bovbjerg, Randall R., and John Holahan (1982), *Medicaid in the Reagan Era,* Washington, D.C.: Urban Institute Press.

Bowden, Ros, and Bill Bunbury (1990), *Being Aboriginal: Comments, Observations and Stories from Aboriginal Australians,* Mayborough, Victoria: Australian Broadcasting Corporation.

Bryant, F. Carlene (1981), *We're All Kin: Cultural Study of a Mountain Neighborhood,* Knoxville: University of Tennessee Press.

Buechner, Jay S., H. Denman Scott, John L. Smith, and Alan B. Humphrey (1991), "WIC Program Participation—A Marketing Approach," *Public Health Reports* 106 (September–October), 247–56.

Caputo, Richard K. (1993), "Family Poverty, Unemployment Rates, and AFDC Payments: Trends among Blacks and Whites," *Journal of Contemporary Human Services* 74 (November), 515–26.

Cromwell, Paul F., James N. Olson, and D'Aunn Wester Avary (1991), *Breaking and Entering: An Ethnographic Analysis of Burglary,* Newbury Park, Calif.: Sage Publications.

Csikszentmihalyi, Mihaly, and Eugene Rochberg-Halton (1981), *The Meaning of Things: Domestic Symbols and the Self,* Cambridge, England: Cambridge University Press.

Cunningham, Patrick M. (1993), *Welfare Reform: A Response to Unemployed Two-Parent Families,* New York: Garland Publishing.

Dasgupta, Partha (1993), *An Inquiry into Well-being and Destitution,* New York: Clarendon Press.

Devaney, Barbara, Linda Bilheimer, and Jennifer Shore (1992), "Medical Costs and Birth Outcomes: The Effects of Prenatal WIC Participation and the Use of Prenatal Care," *Journal of Policy Analysis and Management* 11 (4), 573–92.

Dolbeare, C. N. (1991), *Out of Reach: Why Everyday People Can't Find Affordable Housing,* Washington, D.C.: Low Income Housing Service.

Dornbusch, Sanford (1994), "Additional Perspectives on Homeless Families," *American Behavioral Scientist* 37 (February), 404–11.

Easterlin, Richard E. (1995), "Will Raising the Incomes of All Increase the Happiness of All?" *Journal of Economic Behavior and Organization* 27 (June), 35–47.

Edelman, Marian W., and Lisa Mihaly (1989), "Homeless Families and the Housing Crisis in the United States," *Children and Youth Services Review* 11 (1), 91–108.

Edin, Kathryn (1993), *There's a Lot of Month Left at the End of the Money: How Welfare Recipients Make Ends Meet in Chicago,* New York: Garland Publishing.

Fabricant, Michael (1988), "Empowering the Homeless," *Social Policy* 18 (Spring), 49–55.

Fiene, Judith Ivy (1990), "Snobby People and Just Plain Folks: Social Stratification and Rural Low-Status, Appalachian Women," *Sociological Spectrum* 10, 527–39.

Firat, A. Fuat, and Alladi Venkatesh (1995), "Liberatory Postmodernism and the Reenchantment of Consumption," *Journal of Consumer Research* 22 (December), 239–67.

Franzak, Frank J., Thomas J. Smith, and Christopher E. Desch (1995), "Marketing Cancer Care to Rural Residents," *Journal of Public Policy and Marketing* 14 (Spring), 76–82.

Freeman, Richard B., and Brian Hall (1987), "Permanent Homelessness in America?" *Population and Policy Review* 6, 3–27.

French, Laurence (1987), "Victimization of the Mentally Ill: An Unintended Consequence of Deinstitutionalization," *Social Work* 32 (November–December), 502–5.

Furby, Lita (1979), "Inequities in Personal Possessions: Explanations for and Judgments about Unequal Distribution," *Human Development* 22, 180–202.

Ger, Guliz (1997), "Human Development and Humane Consumption: Well-being Beyond the Good Life," *Journal of Public Policy and Marketing* 16 (Spring), 110–25.

Goffman, Erving (1963), *Stigma: Notes on the Management of Spoiled Identity,* Englewood Cliffs, N.J.: Prentice Hall.

Hagen, Jan L. (1987), "Gender and Homelessness," *Social Work* 32 (4) 312–16.

Hall, Stuart, and T. Jefferson (1991), *Resistance through Rituals,* London: Routledge.

Halpern, Robert (1995), *Rebuilding the Inner City,* New York: Columbia University Press.

Hebdige, Dick (1979), *Subculture: The Meaning of Style,* London: Routledge.

Hill, Ronald Paul (1991), "Health Care and the Homeless: A Marketing-Oriented Approach," *Journal of Health Care Marketing* 11 (June), 14–23.

——— (1994), "The Public Policy Issue of Homelessness: A Review and Synthesis of Existing Research," *Journal of Business Research* 30 (May), 5–12.

Hombs, Mary Ellen, and Mitch Snyder (1983), *Homelessness in America: A Forced March to Nowhere,* Washington, D.C.: Community for Nonviolence.

Honig, Marjorie, and Randall K. Filer (1993), "Causes of Intercity Variations in Homelessness," *American Economic Review* 83 (March), 248–55.

Hopper, Kim, and Jill Hamberg (1985), *The Making of America's Homeless: From Skid Row to the New Poor,* New York: Community Service Society.

Imig, Douglas R. (1996), *Poverty and Power: The Political Representation of Poor Americans,* Lincoln: University of Nebraska Press.

Jencks, Christopher, and Kathryn Edin (1995), "Do Poor Women Have the Right to Bear Children?" *American Prospect* 20 (Winter), 43–52.

Joint Center for Housing Studies of Harvard University (1993), *The State of the Nation's Housing, 1993,* Cambridge: Harvard University Press.

Katz, Jack (1988), *Seduction of Crime: Moral and Sensual Attraction of Doing Evil,* New York: Basic Books.

Klockars, Carl B. (1974), *The Professional Fence,* New York: The Free Press.

Kulis, Stephen (1988), "Emotional Distress Following AFDC Cutbacks," *Social Science Quarterly* 69 (June), 399–415.

Maddock, Kenneth (1972), *The Australian Aborigines: A Portrait of Their Society,* London: Allen Lane.

Marks, Carole (1991), "The Urban Underclass," *Annual Review of Sociology* 17, 445–66.

McCarthy, Bill, and John Hagan (1992), "Mean Streets: The Theoretical Significance of Situational Delinquency among Homeless Youths," *American Journal of Sociology* 98 (November), 597–627.

McCracken, Grant (1988), *Culture and Consumption,* Bloomington: Indiana University Press.

Moffitt, Robert, and Barbara L. Wolfe (1992), "The Effect of the Medicaid Program on Welfare Participation and Labor Supply," *Review of Economics and Statistics* 74 (4), 615–26.

National Mental Health Association (1988), *Homelessness in America,* Washington D.C.: Acropolis.

Peterson, Mark, and Naresh K. Malhotra (1997), "Comparative Marketing Measures of Societal Quality of Life: Substantive Dimensions in 186 Countries," *Journal of Macromarketing* 17 (Spring), 25–38.

Porter, Michael E. (1995), "The Competitive Advantage of the Inner-City," *Harvard Business Review* 73 (May–June), 55–77.

Ringheim, Karen (1990), *At Risk of Homelessness: The Roles of Income and Rent,* New York: Praeger.

Rofuth, Todd W., and Henry Weiss (1991), "Extending Health Care to AFDC Recipients Who Obtain Jobs: Results of a Demonstration," *Health and Social Work* 16 (August), 162–69.

Rogers, Joseph W., and M. D. Buffalo (1974), "Fighting Back: Nine Modes of Adaptation to a Deviant Label," *Social Problems* 22 (October), 101–18.

Ropers, Richard H. (1988), *The Invisible Homeless: A New Urban Ecology,* New York: Human Sciences.

Rossi, Peter (1994), "Troubling Families: Family Homelessness in America," *American Behavioral Scientist* 37 (February), 342–95.

Rossi, Peter H., and James D. Wright (1987), "The Determinants of Homelessness," *Health Affairs* 6 (Spring), 19–32.

Salerno, Dan, Kim Hopper, and Elizabeth Baxter (1984), *Hardship in the Heartland: Homeless in Eight U.S. Cities,* New York: New York Institute for Social Welfare Research, Community Service Society of New York.

Scammon, Debra L., Lawrence B. Li, and Scott D. Williams (1995), "Increasing the Supply of Providers for the Medically Underserved: Marketing and Public Policy Issues," *Journal of Public Policy and Marketing* 14 (Spring), 35–47.

Schaffer, Paul (1998), *Poverty Reduction Strategies: A Review,* New York: United Nations Publications.

Schwendinger, Herman, and Julia Siegel Schwendinger (1985), *Adolescent Subcultures and Delinquency,* New York: Praeger.

Seitz, Virginia Rinaldo (1995), *Women, Development, and Communities for Empowerment in Appalachia,* Albany: State University of New York Press.

Shea, Martina (1995), *Dynamics of Economic Well-being: Poverty, 1990 to 1992,* Washington, D.C.: U.S. Department of Commerce.

Shinn, Marybeth, and Colleen Gillespie (1994), "The Roles of Housing and Poverty in the Origins of Homelessness," *American Behavioral Scientist* 37 (February), 505–21.

Shinn, Marybeth, James Knickman, and Beth Weitzman (1991), "Social Relationships and Vulnerability to Becoming Homeless among Poor Families," *American Psychologist* 46 (11), 1180–1187.

Shinn, Marybeth, and Beth Weitzman (1994), "You Can't Eliminate Homelessness without Housing," *American Behavioral Scientist* 37 (February), 435–42.

Shlay, Anne, and Peter Rossi (1992), "Social Science Research and Contemporary Studies of Homelessness," *Annual Review of Sociology* 18, 129–60.

Shultz, Clifford J. (1997), "Improving Life Quality for the Destitute: Contributions from Multiple-Method Fieldwork in War-Ravaged Transition Economies," *Journal of Macromarketing* 17 (Spring), 56–67.

Shultz, Clifford J., and Anthony Pecotich (1997), "Marketing and Development in the Transition Economies of Southeast Asia: Policy Explication, Assessment, and Implications," *Journal of Public Policy and Marketing* 16 (Spring), 55–68.

Snow, David A., and Leon Anderson (1987), "Identity Work among the Homeless: The Verbal Construction and Avowal of Personal Identities," *American Journal of Sociology* 92 (May), 1336–71.

Snow, David A., Susan G. Baker, Leon Anderson, and Michael Martin (1986), "The Myth of Pervasive Mental Illness among the Homeless," *Social Problems* 33, 407–23.

Snow, David A., and Gerald Bradford (1994), "Broadening Perspectives on Homelessness," *American Behavioral Scientist* 37 (February), 2454–60.

Steffensmeier, Darrell J. (1986), *The Fence: In the Shadow of Two Worlds*, Totowa, N.J.: Rowan & Littlefield.

Streeten, Paul (1994), *Strategies for Human Development: Global Poverty and Unemployment*, Copenhagen: Munksgaard International Publishers.

Vacha, E. F., and M. V. Martin (1993), "Doubling Up: Low Income Households Sheltering the Hidden Homeless," *Journal of Sociology and Social Welfare* 20 (3), 25–41.

Waizkin, Howard (1991), *The Politics of Medical Encounters: How Patients and Doctors Deal with Social Problems*, New Haven: Yale University Press.

Walsh, Marilyn E. (1977), *The Fence*, Westport, Conn.: Greenwood Press.

Weitzman, Beth, James Knickman, and Marybeth Shinn (1990), "Pathways to Homelessness among New York City Families," *Journal of Social Issues* 46 (4), 125–40.

———— (1992), "Predictors of Shelter Use among Low-Income Families: Psychiatric History, Substance Abuse, and Victimization," *American Journal of Public Health* 82 (11), 1547–50.

Willis, Paul E. (1978), *Profane Culture*, London: Routledge & Kegan Paul.

Wilson, William Julius (1996), *When Work Disappears: The World of the New Urban Poor*, New York: Knopf.

Wolfe, Barbara L., and Steven C. Hill (1995), "The Effect of Health on the Work Effort of Single Mothers," *Journal of Human Resources* 30 (Winter), 42–62.

Wright, James, and J. Lamm (1987), "Homelessness and the Low-Income Housing Supply," *Social Policy* 17 (Spring), 48–53.

Wright, James D. (1988), "The Mentally Ill Homeless: What Is Myth and What Is Fact?" *Social Problems* 35 (2), 182–91.